GNU Bash Reference Manual

Reference Documentation for Bash
Edition 3.2, for Bash Version 3.2.
September 2006

Chet Ramey, Case Western Reserve University
Brian Fox, Free Software Foundation
Edited for publication by Brian Gough

Published by Network Theory Ltd.

A catalogue record for this book is available from the British Library.

First printing, December 2002 (27/12/2002).
Second printing (revised for version 3.2), October 2006 (26/10/2006).

Published by Network Theory Limited.

15 Royal Park
Bristol
BS8 3AL
United Kingdom

Email: info@network-theory.co.uk

ISBN 0-9541617-7-7

Further information about this book is available from
http://www.network-theory.co.uk/bash/manual/

This book has an unconditional guarantee. If you are not fully satisfied
with your purchase for any reason, please contact the publisher at the
address above.

The texinfo source files for this manual are available from
http://www.network-theory.co.uk/bash/manual/src/

Table of Contents

Publisher's Preface

This manual documents the use of GNU Bash, a command-line interpreter for the GNU operating system.

GNU Bash is *free software*. The term "free software" is sometimes misunderstood—it has nothing to do with price. It is about freedom. It refers to your freedom to run, copy, distribute, study, change and improve the software. With GNU Bash you have all these freedoms.

GNU Bash is part of the GNU Project. The GNU Project was launched in 1984 to develop a complete Unix-like operating system which is free software: the GNU system. It was conceived as a way of bringing back the cooperative spirit that prevailed in the computing community in earlier days, by removing the obstacles to cooperation imposed by the owners of proprietary software.

The Free Software Foundation is a tax-exempt charity that raises funds for work on the GNU Project and is dedicated to promoting the freedom to modify and redistribute computer programs. You can support the GNU Project by becoming an associate member of the Free Software Foundation and paying regular membership dues. For more information, visit the website www.fsf.org.

Brian Gough
Publisher
October 2006

1 Introduction

1.1 What is Bash?

Bash is the shell, or command language interpreter, for the GNU operating system. The name is an acronym for the 'Bourne-Again SHell', a pun on Stephen Bourne, the author of the direct ancestor of the current Unix shell sh, which appeared in the Seventh Edition Bell Labs Research version of Unix.

Bash is largely compatible with sh and incorporates useful features from the Korn shell ksh and the C shell csh. It is intended to be a conformant implementation of the IEEE POSIX Shell and Tools portion of the IEEE POSIX specification (IEEE Standard 1003.1). It offers functional improvements over sh for both interactive and programming use.

While the GNU operating system provides other shells, including a version of csh, Bash is the default shell. Like other GNU software, Bash is quite portable. It currently runs on nearly every version of Unix and a few other operating systems—independently-supported ports exist for MS-DOS, OS/2, and Windows platforms.

1.2 What is a shell?

At its base, a shell is simply a macro processor that executes commands. The term macro processor means functionality where text and symbols are expanded to create larger expressions.

A Unix shell is both a command interpreter and a programming language. As a command interpreter, the shell provides the user interface to the rich set of GNU utilities. The programming language features allow these utilities to be combined. Files containing commands can be created, and become commands themselves. These new commands have the same status as system commands in directories such as '/bin', allowing users or groups to establish custom environments to automate their common tasks.

Shells may be used interactively or non-interactively. In interactive mode, they accept input typed from the keyboard. When executing non-interactively, shells execute commands read from a file.

A shell allows execution of GNU commands, both synchronously and asynchronously. The shell waits for synchronous commands to complete before accepting more input; asynchronous commands continue to execute in parallel with the shell while it reads and executes additional commands.

The *redirection* constructs permit fine-grained control of the input and output of those commands. Moreover, the shell allows control over the contents of commands' environments.

Shells also provide a small set of built-in commands (*builtins*) implementing functionality impossible or inconvenient to obtain via separate utilities. For example, cd, break, continue, and exec) cannot be implemented outside of the shell because they directly manipulate the shell itself. The history, getopts, kill, or pwd builtins, among others, could be implemented in separate utilities, but they are more convenient to use as builtin commands. All of the shell builtins are described in subsequent sections.

While executing commands is essential, most of the power (and complexity) of shells is due to their embedded programming languages. Like any high-level language, the shell provides variables, flow control constructs, quoting, and functions.

Shells offer features geared specifically for interactive use rather than to augment the programming language. These interactive features include job control, command line editing, command history and aliases. Each of these features is described in this manual.

2 Definitions

These definitions are used throughout the remainder of this manual.

POSIX
: A family of open system standards based on Unix. Bash is primarily concerned with the Shell and Utilities portion of the POSIX 1003.1 standard.

blank
: A space or tab character.

builtin
: A command that is implemented internally by the shell itself, rather than by an executable program somewhere in the file system.

control operator
: A word that performs a control function. It is a newline or one of the following: '||', '&&', '&', ';', ';;', '|', '(', or ')'.

exit status
: The value returned by a command to its caller. The value is restricted to eight bits, so the maximum value is 255.

field
: A unit of text that is the result of one of the shell expansions. After expansion, when executing a command, the resulting fields are used as the command name and arguments.

filename
: A string of characters used to identify a file.

job
: A set of processes comprising a pipeline, and any processes descended from it, that are all in the same process group.

job control
: A mechanism by which users can selectively stop (suspend) and restart (resume) execution of processes.

metacharacter
: A character that, when unquoted, separates words. A metacharacter is a blank or one of the following characters: '|', '&', ';', '(', ')', '<', or '>'.

name
: A word consisting solely of letters, numbers, and underscores, and beginning with a letter or underscore. Names are used as shell variable and function names. Also referred to as an identifier.

operator
: A control operator or a redirection operator. See Section 3.6 [Redirections], page 32, for a list of redirection operators.

process group
> A collection of related processes each having the same process group ID.

process group ID
> A unique identifier that represents a process group during its lifetime.

reserved word
> A word that has a special meaning to the shell. Most reserved words introduce shell flow control constructs, such as `for` and `while`.

return status
> A synonym for `exit status`.

signal
> A mechanism by which a process may be notified by the kernel of an event occurring in the system.

special builtin
> A shell builtin command that has been classified as special by the POSIX standard.

token
> A sequence of characters considered a single unit by the shell. It is either a `word` or an `operator`.

word
> A `token` that is not an operator.

3 Basic Shell Features

Bash is an acronym for 'Bourne-Again SHell'. The Bourne shell is the traditional Unix shell originally written by Stephen Bourne. All of the Bourne shell builtin commands are available in Bash, The rules for evaluation and quoting are taken from the POSIX specification for the 'standard' Unix shell.

This chapter briefly summarizes the shell's 'building blocks': commands, control structures, shell functions, shell *parameters*, shell expansions, *redirections*, which are a way to direct input and output from and to named files, and how the shell executes commands.

3.1 Shell Syntax

When the shell reads input, it proceeds through a sequence of operations. If the input indicates the beginning of a comment, the shell ignores the comment symbol ('#'), and the rest of that line.

Otherwise, roughly speaking, the shell reads its input and divides the input into words and operators, employing the quoting rules to select which meanings to assign various words and characters.

The shell then parses these tokens into commands and other constructs, removes the special meaning of certain words or characters, expands others, redirects input and output as needed, executes the specified command, waits for the command's exit status, and makes that exit status available for further inspection or processing.

3.1.1 Shell Operation

The following is a brief description of the shell's operation when it reads and executes a command. Basically, the shell does the following:

1. Reads its input from a file (see Section 3.8 [Shell Scripts], page 41), from a string supplied as an argument to the '-c' invocation option (see Section 6.1 [Invoking Bash], page 85), or from the user's terminal.

2. Breaks the input into words and operators, obeying the quoting rules described in Section 3.1.2 [Quoting], page 8. These tokens are separated by metacharacters. Alias expansion is performed by this step (see Section 6.6 [Aliases], page 95).

3. Parses the tokens into simple and compound commands (see Section 3.2 [Shell Commands], page 10).

4. Performs the various shell expansions (see Section 3.5 [Shell Expansions], page 22), breaking the expanded tokens into lists of filenames (see Section 3.5.8 [Filename Expansion], page 30) and commands and arguments.

5. Performs any necessary redirections (see Section 3.6 [Redirections], page 32) and removes the redirection operators and their operands from the argument list.

6. Executes the command (see Section 3.7 [Executing Commands], page 36).

7. Optionally waits for the command to complete and collects its exit status (see Section 3.7.5 [Exit Status], page 40).

3.1.2 Quoting

Quoting is used to remove the special meaning of certain characters or words to the shell. Quoting can be used to disable special treatment for special characters, to prevent reserved words from being recognized as such, and to prevent parameter expansion.

Each of the shell metacharacters (see Chapter 2 [Definitions], page 5) has special meaning to the shell and must be quoted if it is to represent itself. When the command history expansion facilities are being used (see Section 9.3 [History Interaction], page 147), the *history expansion* character, usually '!', must be quoted to prevent history expansion. See Section 9.1 [Bash History Facilities], page 145, for more details concerning history expansion.

There are three quoting mechanisms: the *escape character*, single quotes, and double quotes.

3.1.2.1 Escape Character

A non-quoted backslash '\' is the Bash escape character. It preserves the literal value of the next character that follows, with the exception of newline. If a \newline pair appears, and the backslash itself is not quoted, the \newline is treated as a line continuation (that is, it is removed from the input stream and effectively ignored).

3.1.2.2 Single Quotes

Enclosing characters in single quotes (''') preserves the literal value of each character within the quotes. A single quote may not occur between single quotes, even when preceded by a backslash.

3.1.2.3 Double Quotes

Enclosing characters in double quotes ('"') preserves the literal value of all characters within the quotes, with the exception of '$', '`', '\', and, when history expansion is enabled, '!'. The characters '$' and '`' retain their special meaning within double quotes (see Section 3.5 [Shell Expansions], page 22). The backslash retains its special meaning only when followed by one of the following characters: '$', '`', '"', '\', or newline. Within double quotes, backslashes that are followed by one of these characters are removed. Backslashes preceding characters without a special meaning are left unmodified. A double quote may be quoted within double quotes by preceding it with a backslash. If enabled, history expansion will be performed unless an '!' appearing in double quotes is escaped using a backslash. The backslash preceding the '!' is not removed.

The special parameters '*' and '@' have special meaning when in double quotes (see Section 3.5.3 [Shell Parameter Expansion], page 25).

3.1.2.4 ANSI-C Quoting

Words of the form $'*string*' are treated specially. The word expands to *string*, with backslash-escaped characters replaced as specified by the ANSI C standard. Backslash escape sequences, if present, are decoded as follows:

\a   alert (bell)

\b   backspace

\e   an escape character (not ANSI C)

\f   form feed

\n   newline

\r   carriage return

\t   horizontal tab

\v   vertical tab

\\   backslash

\'   single quote

nnn   the eight-bit character whose value is the octal value *nnn* (one to three digits)

\x*HH*   the eight-bit character whose value is the hexadecimal value *HH* (one or two hex digits)

\cx   a control-x character

The expanded result is single-quoted, as if the dollar sign had not been present.

3.1.2.5 Locale-Specific Translation

A double-quoted string preceded by a dollar sign ('$') will cause the string to be translated according to the current locale. If the current locale is C or POSIX, the dollar sign is ignored. If the string is translated and replaced, the replacement is double-quoted.

Some systems use the message catalog selected by the LC_MESSAGES shell variable. Others create the name of the message catalog from the value of the TEXTDOMAIN shell variable, possibly adding a suffix of '.mo'. If you use the TEXTDOMAIN variable, you may need to set the TEXTDOMAINDIR variable to the location of the message catalog files. Still others use both variables in this fashion: TEXTDOMAINDIR/LC_MESSAGES/LC_MESSAGES/TEXTDOMAIN.mo.

3.1.3 Comments

In a non-interactive shell, or an interactive shell in which the interactive_comments option to the shopt builtin is enabled (see Section 4.2 [Bash Builtins], page 51), a word beginning with '#' causes that word and all remaining characters on that line to be ignored. An interactive shell without the interactive_comments option enabled does not allow comments. The interactive_comments option is on by default in interactive shells. See Section 6.3 [Interactive Shells], page 90, for a description of what makes a shell interactive.

3.2 Shell Commands

A simple shell command such as echo a b c consists of the command itself followed by arguments, separated by spaces.

More complex shell commands are composed of simple commands arranged together in a variety of ways: in a pipeline in which the output of one command becomes the input of a second, in a loop or conditional construct, or in some other grouping.

3.2.1 Simple Commands

A simple command is the kind of command encountered most often. It's just a sequence of words separated by blanks, terminated by one of the shell's control operators (see Chapter 2 [Definitions], page 5). The first word generally specifies a command to be executed, with the rest of the words being that command's arguments.

The return status (see Section 3.7.5 [Exit Status], page 40) of a simple command is its exit status as provided by the POSIX 1003.1 waitpid function, or 128+n if the command was terminated by signal n.

3.2.2 Pipelines

A pipeline is a sequence of simple commands separated by '|'.

The format for a pipeline is

```
[time [-p]] [!] command1 [| command2 ...]
```

The output of each command in the pipeline is connected via a pipe to the input of the next command. That is, each command reads the previous command's output.

The reserved word time causes timing statistics to be printed for the pipeline once it finishes. The statistics currently consist of elapsed (wall-clock) time and user and system time consumed by the command's execution. The '-p' option changes the output format to that specified by POSIX. The TIMEFORMAT variable may be set to a format string that specifies how the timing information should be displayed. See Section 5.2 [Bash Variables], page 74, for a description of the available formats. The use of time as a reserved word permits the timing of shell builtins, shell functions, and pipelines. An external time command cannot time these easily.

If the pipeline is not executed asynchronously (see Section 3.2.3 [Lists], page 12), the shell waits for all commands in the pipeline to complete.

Each command in a pipeline is executed in its own subshell (see Section 3.7.3 [Command Execution Environment], page 38). The exit status of a pipeline is the exit status of the last command in the pipeline, unless the pipefail option is enabled (see Section 4.3 [The Set Builtin], page 66). If pipefail is enabled, the pipeline's return status is the value of the last (rightmost) command to exit with a non-zero status, or zero if all commands exit successfully. If the reserved word '!' precedes the pipeline, the exit status is the logical negation of the exit status as described above. The shell waits for all commands in the pipeline to terminate before returning a value.

3.2.3 Lists of Commands

A list is a sequence of one or more pipelines separated by one of the operators ';', '&', '&&', or '||', and optionally terminated by one of ';', '&', or a newline.

Of these list operators, '&&' and '||' have equal precedence, followed by ';' and '&', which have equal precedence.

A sequence of one or more newlines may appear in a list to delimit commands, equivalent to a semicolon.

If a command is terminated by the control operator '&', the shell executes the command asynchronously in a subshell. This is known as executing the command in the *background*. The shell does not wait for the command to finish, and the return status is 0 (true). When job control is not active (see Chapter 7 [Job Control], page 107), the standard input for asynchronous commands, in the absence of any explicit redirections, is redirected from /dev/null.

Commands separated by a ';' are executed sequentially; the shell waits for each command to terminate in turn. The return status is the exit status of the last command executed.

The control operators '&&' and '||' denote AND lists and OR lists, respectively. An AND list has the form

    command1 && *command2*

command2 is executed if, and only if, *command1* returns an exit status of zero.

An OR list has the form

    command1 || *command2*

command2 is executed if, and only if, *command1* returns a non-zero exit status.

The return status of AND and OR lists is the exit status of the last command executed in the list.

3.2.4 Compound Commands

Compound commands are the shell programming constructs. Each construct begins with a reserved word or control operator and is terminated by a corresponding reserved word or operator. Any redirections (see Section 3.6 [Redirections], page 32) associated with a compound command apply to all commands within that compound command unless explicitly overridden.

Bash provides looping constructs, conditional commands, and mechanisms to group commands and execute them as a unit.

3.2.4.1 Looping Constructs

Bash supports the following looping constructs.

Note that wherever a ';' appears in the description of a command's syntax, it may be replaced with one or more newlines.

until   The syntax of the until command is:

> until *test-commands*; do
>   *consequent-commands*;
> done

Execute *consequent-commands* as long as *test-commands* has an exit status which is not zero. The return status is the exit status of the last command executed in *consequent-commands*, or zero if none was executed.

while   The syntax of the while command is:

> while *test-commands*; do
>   *consequent-commands*;
> done

Execute *consequent-commands* as long as *test-commands* has an exit status of zero. The return status is the exit status of the last command executed in *consequent-commands*, or zero if none was executed.

for   The syntax of the for command is:

> for *name* [in *words* ...]; do
>   *commands*;
> done

Expand *words*, and execute *commands* once for each member in the resultant list, with *name* bound to the current member. If 'in *words*' is not present, the for command executes the *commands* once for each positional parameter that is set, as if 'in "$@"' had been specified (see Section 3.4.2 [Special Parameters], page 21). The return status is the exit status of the last command that executes. If there are no items in the expansion of *words*, no commands are executed, and the return status is zero.

An alternate form of the for command is also supported:

> for ((*expr1* ; *expr2* ; *expr3*)) ; do
>   *commands* ;
> done

First, the arithmetic expression *expr1* is evaluated according to the rules described below (see Section 6.5 [Shell Arith-

metic], page 94). The arithmetic expression *expr2* is then
evaluated repeatedly until it evaluates to zero. Each time
expr2 evaluates to a non-zero value, *commands* are executed
and the arithmetic expression *expr3* is evaluated. If any expression is omitted, it behaves as if it evaluates to 1. The
return value is the exit status of the last command in *list*
that is executed, or false if any of the expressions is invalid.

The break and continue builtins (see Section 4.1 [Bourne Shell
Builtins], page 43) may be used to control loop execution.

3.2.4.2 Conditional Constructs

if   The syntax of the if command is:

                    if *test-commands*; then
                        consequent-commands;
                    [elif *more-test-commands*; then
                        more-consequents;]
                    [else *alternate-consequents*;]
                    fi

                The *test-commands* list is executed, and if its return sta-
                tus is zero, the *consequent-commands* list is executed. If
                test-commands returns a non-zero status, each elif list is
                executed in turn, and if its exit status is zero, the corre-
                sponding *more-consequents* is executed and the command
                completes. If 'else *alternate-consequents*' is present, and
                the final command in the final if or elif clause has a non-
                zero exit status, then *alternate-consequents* is executed. The
                return status is the exit status of the last command executed,
                or zero if no condition tested true.

case   The syntax of the case command is:

                    case *word* in
                        [[(] *pattern* [| *pattern*]...) *command-list* ;;]
                        ...
                    esac

                case will selectively execute the *command-list* corresponding
                to the first *pattern* that matches *word*. If the shell option
                nocasematch (see the description of shopt in Section 4.2
                [Bash Builtins], page 51) is enabled, the match is performed
                without regard to the case of alphabetic characters. The '|'
                is used to separate multiple patterns, and the ')' operator

terminates a pattern list. A list of patterns and an associated command-list is known as a *clause*. Each clause must be terminated with '; ;'. The *word* undergoes tilde expansion, parameter expansion, command substitution, arithmetic expansion, and quote removal before matching is attempted. Each *pattern* undergoes tilde expansion, parameter expansion, command substitution, and arithmetic expansion.

There may be an arbitrary number of case clauses, each terminated by a '; ;'. The first pattern that matches determines the command-list that is executed.

Here is an example using case in a script that could be used to describe one interesting feature of an animal:

```
echo -n "Enter the name of an animal: "
read ANIMAL
echo -n "The $ANIMAL has "
case $ANIMAL in
   horse | dog | cat) echo -n "four";;
   man | kangaroo ) echo -n "two";;
   *) echo -n "an unknown number of";;
esac
echo " legs."
```

The return status is zero if no *pattern* is matched. Otherwise, the return status is the exit status of the *command-list* executed.

select

The select construct allows the easy generation of menus. It has almost the same syntax as the for command:

```
select name [in words ...]; do
   commands;
done
```

The list of words following in is expanded, generating a list of items. The set of expanded words is printed on the standard error output stream, each preceded by a number. If the 'in *words*' is omitted, the positional parameters are printed, as if 'in "$@"' had been specified. The PS3 prompt is then displayed and a line is read from the standard input. If the line consists of a number corresponding to one of the displayed words, then the value of *name* is set to that word. If the line is empty, the words and prompt are displayed again. If EOF is read, the select command completes. Any other value read causes *name* to be set to null. The line read is saved in the variable REPLY.

The *commands* are executed after each selection until a break command is executed, at which point the select command completes.

Here is an example that allows the user to pick a filename from the current directory, and displays the name and index of the file selected.

```
select fname in *;
do
echo you picked $fname \($REPLY\)
break;
done
```

((...))

        ((*expression*))

The arithmetic *expression* is evaluated according to the rules described below (see Section 6.5 [Shell Arithmetic], page 94). If the value of the expression is non-zero, the return status is 0; otherwise the return status is 1. This is exactly equivalent to

        let "*expression*"

See Section 4.2 [Bash Builtins], page 51, for a full description of the let builtin.

[[...]]

        [[*expression*]]

Return a status of 0 or 1 depending on the evaluation of the conditional expression *expression*. Expressions are composed of the primaries described below in Section 6.4 [Bash Conditional Expressions], page 92. Word splitting and filename expansion are not performed on the words between the '[[' and ']]'; tilde expansion, parameter and variable expansion, arithmetic expansion, command substitution, process substitution, and quote removal are performed. Conditional operators such as '-f' must be unquoted to be recognized as primaries.

When the '==' and '!=' operators are used, the string to the right of the operator is considered a pattern and matched according to the rules described below in Section 3.5.8.1 [Pattern Matching], page 31. If the shell option nocasematch (see the description of shopt in Section 4.2 [Bash Builtins], page 51) is enabled, the match is performed without regard to the case of alphabetic characters. The return value is 0 if the string matches ('==') or does not match ('!=')the pattern, and 1 otherwise. Any part of the pattern may be quoted to force it to be matched as a string.

An additional binary operator, '=~', is available, with the same precedence as '==' and '!='. When it is used, the string to the right of the operator is considered an extended regular expression and matched accordingly (as in *regex*3)). The return value is 0 if the string matches the pattern, and 1 otherwise. If the regular expression is syntactically incorrect, the conditional expression's return value is 2. If the shell option nocasematch (see the description of shopt in Section 4.2 [Bash Builtins], page 51) is enabled, the match is performed without regard to the case of alphabetic characters. Substrings matched by parenthesized subexpressions within the regular expression are saved in the array variable BASH_REMATCH. The element of BASH_REMATCH with index 0 is the portion of the string matching the entire regular expression. The element of BASH_REMATCH with index *n* is the portion of the string matching the *n*th parenthesized subexpression.

Expressions may be combined using the following operators, listed in decreasing order of precedence:

(*expression*)

>Returns the value of *expression*. This may be used to override the normal precedence of operators.

! *expression*

>True if *expression* is false.

expression1 && *expression2*

>True if both *expression1* and *expression2* are true.

expression1 || *expression2*

>True if either *expression1* or *expression2* is true.

The && and || operators do not evaluate *expression2* if the value of *expression1* is sufficient to determine the return value of the entire conditional expression.

3.2.4.3 Grouping Commands

Bash provides two ways to group a list of commands to be executed as a unit. When commands are grouped, redirections may be applied to the entire command list. For example, the output of all the commands in the list may be redirected to a single stream.

()

>   (*list*)

>   Placing a list of commands between parentheses causes a subshell environment to be created (see Section 3.7.3 [Command Execution Environment], page 38), and each of the commands in *list* to be executed in that subshell. Since the *list* is executed in a subshell, variable assignments do not remain in effect after the subshell completes.

{}

>   { *list*; }

>   Placing a list of commands between curly braces causes the list to be executed in the current shell context. No subshell is created. The semicolon (or newline) following *list* is required.

In addition to the creation of a subshell, there is a subtle difference between these two constructs due to historical reasons. The braces are reserved words, so they must be separated from the *list* by blanks. The parentheses are operators, and are recognized as separate tokens by the shell even if they are not separated from the *list* by whitespace.

The exit status of both of these constructs is the exit status of *list*.

3.3 Shell Functions

Shell functions are a way to group commands for later execution using a single name for the group. They are executed just like a "regular" command. When the name of a shell function is used as a simple command name, the list of commands associated with that function name is executed. Shell functions are executed in the current shell context; no new process is created to interpret them.

Functions are declared using this syntax:

[function] *name* () *compound-command* [*redirections*]

This defines a shell function named *name*. The reserved word function is optional. If the function reserved word is supplied, the parentheses are optional. The *body* of the function is the compound command *compound-command* (see Section 3.2.4 [Compound Commands], page 12). That command is usually a *list* enclosed between { and }, but may be any compound command listed above. *compound-command* is executed whenever *name* is specified as the name of a command. Any redirections (see Section 3.6 [Redirections], page 32) associated with the shell function are performed when the function is executed.

A function definition may be deleted using the '-f' option to the unset builtin (see Section 4.1 [Bourne Shell Builtins], page 43).

The exit status of a function definition is zero unless a syntax error occurs or a readonly function with the same name already exists. When executed, the exit status of a function is the exit status of the last command executed in the body.

Note that for historical reasons, in the most common usage the curly braces that surround the body of the function must be separated from the body by blanks or newlines. This is because the braces are reserved words and are only recognized as such when they are separated by whitespace. Also, when using the braces, the *list* must be terminated by a semicolon, an ampersand '&', or a newline.

When a function is executed, the arguments to the function become the positional parameters during its execution (see Section 3.4.1 [Positional Parameters], page 21). The special parameter '#' that expands to the number of positional parameters is updated to reflect the change. Special parameter 0 is unchanged. The first element of the FUNCNAME variable is set to the name of the function while the function is executing. All other aspects of the shell execution environment are identical between a function and its caller with the exception that the DEBUG and RETURN traps are not inherited unless the function has been given the trace attribute using the declare builtin or the -o functrace option has been enabled with the set builtin, (in which case all functions inherit the DEBUG and RETURN traps). See Section 4.1 [Bourne Shell Builtins], page 43, for the description of the trap builtin.

If the builtin command return is executed in a function, the function completes and execution resumes with the next command after the function call. Any command associated with the RETURN trap is executed before execution resumes. When a function completes, the values of the positional parameters and the special parameter '#' are restored to the values they had prior to the function's execution. If a numeric argument is given to return, that is the function's return status; otherwise the function's return status is the exit status of the last command executed before the return.

Variables local to the function may be declared with the local builtin. These variables are visible only to the function and the commands it invokes.

Function names and definitions may be listed with the '-f' option to the declare or typeset builtin commands (see Section 4.2 [Bash Builtins], page 51). The '-F' option to declare or typeset will list the function names only (and optionally the source file and line number, if the extdebug shell option is enabled). Functions may be exported so that subshells automatically have them defined with the '-f' option to the export builtin (see Section 4.1 [Bourne Shell Builtins], page 43). Note that shell functions and variables with the same name may result in multiple identically-named entries in the environment passed to the shell's children. Care should be taken in cases where this may cause a problem.

Functions may be recursive. No limit is placed on the number of recursive calls.

3.4 Shell Parameters

A *parameter* is an entity that stores values. It can be a name, a number, or one of the special characters listed below. A *variable* is a parameter denoted by a name. A variable has a *value* and zero or more *attributes*. Attributes are assigned using the declare builtin command (see the description of the declare builtin in Section 4.2 [Bash Builtins], page 51).

A parameter is set if it has been assigned a value. The null string is a valid value. Once a variable is set, it may be unset only by using the unset builtin command.

A variable may be assigned to by a statement of the form

    name=[*value*]

If *value* is not given, the variable is assigned the null string. All *values* undergo tilde expansion, parameter and variable expansion, command substitution, arithmetic expansion, and quote removal (detailed below). If the variable has its integer attribute set, then *value* is evaluated as an arithmetic expression even if the $((...)) expansion is not used (see Section 3.5.5 [Arithmetic Expansion], page 29). Word splitting is not performed, with the exception of "$@" as explained below. Filename expansion is not performed. Assignment statements may also appear as arguments to the alias, declare, typeset, export, readonly, and local builtin commands.

In the context where an assignment statement is assigning a value to a shell variable or array index (see Section 6.7 [Arrays], page 96), the '+=' operator can be used to append to or add to the variable's previous value. When '+=' is applied to a variable for which the integer attribute has been set, *value* is evaluated as an arithmetic expression and added to the variable's current value, which is also evaluated. When '+=' is applied to an array variable using compound assignment (see Section 6.7 [Arrays], page 96), the variable's value is not unset (as it is when using '='), and new values are appended to the array beginning at one greater than the array's maximum index. When applied to a string-valued variable, *value* is expanded and appended to the variable's value.

3.4.1 Positional Parameters

A *positional parameter* is a parameter denoted by one or more digits, other than the single digit 0. Positional parameters are assigned from the shell's arguments when it is invoked, and may be reassigned using the set builtin command. Positional parameter N may be referenced as ${N}, or as $N when N consists of a single digit. Positional parameters may not be assigned to with assignment statements. The set and shift builtins are used to set and unset them (see Chapter 4 [Shell Builtin Commands], page 43). The positional parameters are temporarily replaced when a shell function is executed (see Section 3.3 [Shell Functions], page 18).

When a positional parameter consisting of more than a single digit is expanded, it must be enclosed in braces.

3.4.2 Special Parameters

The shell treats several parameters specially. These parameters may only be referenced; assignment to them is not allowed.

*   Expands to the positional parameters, starting from one. When the expansion occurs within double quotes, it expands to a single word with the value of each parameter separated by the first character of the IFS special variable. That is, "$*" is equivalent to "$1c$2c...", where c is the first character of the value of the IFS variable. If IFS is unset, the parameters are separated by spaces. If IFS is null, the parameters are joined without intervening separators.

@   Expands to the positional parameters, starting from one. When the expansion occurs within double quotes, each parameter expands to a separate word. That is, "$@" is equivalent to "$1" "$2" .... If the double-quoted expansion occurs within a word, the expansion of the first parameter is joined with the beginning part of the original word, and the expansion of the last parameter is joined with the last part of the original word. When there are no positional parameters, "$@" and $@ expand to nothing (i.e., they are removed).

Expands to the number of positional parameters in decimal.

?   Expands to the exit status of the most recently executed
                foreground pipeline.

-               (A hyphen.) Expands to the current option flags as specified
                upon invocation, by the set builtin command, or those set
                by the shell itself (such as the '-i' option).

$ Expands to the process ID of the shell. In a () subshell,
                it expands to the process ID of the invoking shell, not the
                subshell.

!   Expands to the process ID of the most recently executed
                background (asynchronous) command.

0   Expands to the name of the shell or shell script. This is
                set at shell initialization. If Bash is invoked with a file of
                commands (see Section 3.8 [Shell Scripts], page 41), $0 is
                set to the name of that file. If Bash is started with the '-c'
                option (see Section 6.1 [Invoking Bash], page 85), then $0 is
                set to the first argument after the string to be executed, if
                one is present. Otherwise, it is set to the filename used to
                invoke Bash, as given by argument zero.

_   (An underscore.) At shell startup, set to the absolute path-
                name used to invoke the shell or shell script being executed
                as passed in the environment or argument list. Subsequently,
                expands to the last argument to the previous command, after
                expansion. Also set to the full pathname used to invoke each
                command executed and placed in the environment exported
                to that command. When checking mail, this parameter holds
                the name of the mail file.

3.5 Shell Expansions

Expansion is performed on the command line after it has been split
into tokens. There are seven kinds of expansion performed:

- brace expansion
- tilde expansion
- parameter and variable expansion
- command substitution
- arithmetic expansion
- word splitting
- filename expansion

The order of expansions is: brace expansion, tilde expansion, parameter, variable, and arithmetic expansion and command substitution (done in a left-to-right fashion), word splitting, and filename expansion.

On systems that can support it, there is an additional expansion available: *process substitution*. This is performed at the same time as parameter, variable, and arithmetic expansion and command substitution.

Only brace expansion, word splitting, and filename expansion can change the number of words of the expansion; other expansions expand a single word to a single word. The only exceptions to this are the expansions of "$@" (see Section 3.4.2 [Special Parameters], page 21) and "${name[@]}" (see Section 6.7 [Arrays], page 96).

After all expansions, quote removal (see Section 3.5.9 [Quote Removal], page 32) is performed.

3.5.1 Brace Expansion

Brace expansion is a mechanism by which arbitrary strings may be generated. This mechanism is similar to *filename expansion* (see Section 3.5.8 [Filename Expansion], page 30), but the file names generated need not exist. Patterns to be brace expanded take the form of an optional *preamble*, followed by either a series of comma-separated strings or a sequence expression between a pair of braces, followed by an optional *postscript*. The preamble is prefixed to each string contained within the braces, and the postscript is then appended to each resulting string, expanding left to right.

Brace expansions may be nested. The results of each expanded string are not sorted; left to right order is preserved. For example,

```
bash$ echo a{d,c,b}e
ade ace abe
```

A sequence expression takes the form $\{x..y\}$, where x and y are either integers or single characters. When integers are supplied, the expression expands to each number between x and y, inclusive. When characters are supplied, the expression expands to each character lexicographically between x and y, inclusive. Note that both x and y must be of the same type.

Brace expansion is performed before any other expansions, and any characters special to other expansions are preserved in the result. It is strictly textual. Bash does not apply any syntactic interpretation to the context of the expansion or the text between the braces. To avoid conflicts with parameter expansion, the string '${' is not considered eligible for brace expansion.

A correctly-formed brace expansion must contain unquoted opening and closing braces, and at least one unquoted comma or a valid sequence expression. Any incorrectly formed brace expansion is left unchanged.

A { or ',' may be quoted with a backslash to prevent its being considered part of a brace expression. To avoid conflicts with parameter expansion, the string '${' is not considered eligible for brace expansion.

This construct is typically used as shorthand when the common prefix of the strings to be generated is longer than in the above example:

```
mkdir /usr/local/src/bash/{old,new,dist,bugs}
```
or
```
chown root /usr/{ucb/{ex,edit},lib/{ex?.?*,how_ex}}
```

3.5.2 Tilde Expansion

If a word begins with an unquoted tilde character ('~'), all of the characters up to the first unquoted slash (or all characters, if there is no unquoted slash) are considered a *tilde-prefix*. If none of the characters in the tilde-prefix are quoted, the characters in the tilde-prefix following the tilde are treated as a possible *login name*. If this login name is the null string, the tilde is replaced with the value of the HOME shell variable. If HOME is unset, the home directory of the user executing the shell is substituted instead. Otherwise, the tilde-prefix is replaced with the home directory associated with the specified login name.

If the tilde-prefix is '~+', the value of the shell variable PWD replaces the tilde-prefix. If the tilde-prefix is '~-', the value of the shell variable OLDPWD, if it is set, is substituted.

If the characters following the tilde in the tilde-prefix consist of a number N, optionally prefixed by a '+' or a '-', the tilde-prefix is replaced with the corresponding element from the directory stack, as it would be displayed by the dirs builtin invoked with the characters following tilde in the tilde-prefix as an argument (see Section 6.8 [The Directory Stack], page 98). If the tilde-prefix, sans the tilde, consists of a number without a leading '+' or '-', '+' is assumed.

If the login name is invalid, or the tilde expansion fails, the word is left unchanged.

Each variable assignment is checked for unquoted tilde-prefixes immediately following a ':' or the first '='. In these cases, tilde expansion is also performed. Consequently, one may use file names with tildes in assignments to PATH, MAILPATH, and CDPATH, and the shell assigns the expanded value.

The following table shows how Bash treats unquoted tilde-prefixes:

~   The value of $HOME

~/foo   '$HOME/foo'

~fred/foo   The subdirectory foo of the home directory of the user fred

~+/foo   '$PWD/foo'

~-/foo   '${OLDPWD-'~-'}/foo'

~N The string that would be displayed by 'dirs +N'

~+N The string that would be displayed by 'dirs +N'

~-N The string that would be displayed by 'dirs -N'

3.5.3 Shell Parameter Expansion

The '$' character introduces parameter expansion, command substi-
tution, or arithmetic expansion. The parameter name or symbol to be
expanded may be enclosed in braces, which are optional but serve to pro-
tect the variable to be expanded from characters immediately following it
which could be interpreted as part of the name.

When braces are used, the matching ending brace is the first '}' not
escaped by a backslash or within a quoted string, and not within an
embedded arithmetic expansion, command substitution, or parameter expansion.

The basic form of parameter expansion is ${*parameter*}. The value
of *parameter* is substituted. The braces are required when *parameter* is
a positional parameter with more than one digit, or when *parameter* is
followed by a character that is not to be interpreted as part of its name.

If the first character of *parameter* is an exclamation point, a level
of variable indirection is introduced. Bash uses the value of the variable formed from the rest of *parameter* as the name of the variable; this
variable is then expanded and that value is used in the rest of the substitution, rather than the value of *parameter* itself. This is known as indirect
expansion. The exceptions to this are the expansions of ${!*prefix**} and
${!*name*[@]} described below. The exclamation point must immediately
follow the left brace in order to introduce indirection.

In each of the cases below, *word* is subject to tilde expansion, parameter expansion, command substitution, and arithmetic expansion.

When not performing substring expansion, Bash tests for a parameter that is unset or null; omitting the colon results in a test only for a
parameter that is unset. Put another way, if the colon is included, the
operator tests for both existence and that the value is not null; if the colon
is omitted, the operator tests only for existence.

${parameter : − word}

> If *parameter* is unset or null, the expansion of *word* is substituted. Otherwise, the value of *parameter* is substituted.

${parameter : = word}

> If *parameter* is unset or null, the expansion of *word* is assigned to *parameter*. The value of *parameter* is then substituted. Positional parameters and special parameters may not be assigned to in this way.

${parameter : ? word}

> If *parameter* is null or unset, the expansion of *word* (or a message to that effect if *word* is not present) is written to the standard error and the shell, if it is not interactive, exits. Otherwise, the value of *parameter* is substituted.

${parameter : + word}

> If *parameter* is null or unset, nothing is substituted, otherwise the expansion of *word* is substituted.

${parameter : offset}
${parameter : offset : length}

> Expands to up to *length* characters of *parameter* starting at the character specified by *offset*. If *length* is omitted, expands to the substring of *parameter* starting at the character specified by *offset*. *length* and *offset* are arithmetic expressions (see Section 6.5 [Shell Arithmetic], page 94). This is referred to as Substring Expansion.
>
> *length* must evaluate to a number greater than or equal to zero. If *offset* evaluates to a number less than zero, the value is used as an offset from the end of the value of *parameter*. If *parameter* is '@', the result is *length* positional parameters beginning at *offset*. If *parameter* is an array name indexed by '@' or '*', the result is the *length* members of the array beginning with ${parameter [offset] }. A negative *offset* is taken relative to one greater than the maximum index of the specified array. Note that a negative offset must be separated from the colon by at least one space to avoid being confused with the ':-' expansion. Substring indexing is zero-based unless the positional parameters are used, in which case the indexing starts at 1.

${!*prefix**}
${!*prefix*@}

> Expands to the names of variables whose names begin with *prefix*, separated by the first character of the IFS special variable.

${!*name*[@]}
${!*name*[*]}

> If *name* is an array variable, expands to the list of array indices (keys) assigned in *name*. If *name* is not an array, expands to 0 if *name* is set and null otherwise. When '@' is used and the expansion appears within double quotes, each key expands to a separate word.

${#*parameter*}

> The length in characters of the expanded value of *parameter* is substituted. If *parameter* is '*' or '@', the value substituted is the number of positional parameters. If *parameter* is an array name subscripted by '*' or '@', the value substituted is the number of elements in the array.

${*parameter*#*word*}
${*parameter*##*word*}

> The *word* is expanded to produce a pattern just as in filename expansion (see Section 3.5.8 [Filename Expansion], page 30). If the pattern matches the beginning of the expanded value of *parameter*, then the result of the expansion is the expanded value of *parameter* with the shortest matching pattern (the '#' case) or the longest matching pattern (the '##' case) deleted. If *parameter* is '@' or '*', the pattern removal operation is applied to each positional parameter in turn, and the expansion is the resultant list. If *parameter* is an array variable subscripted with '@' or '*', the pattern removal operation is applied to each member of the array in turn, and the expansion is the resultant list.

${*parameter*%*word*}
${*parameter*%%*word*}

> The *word* is expanded to produce a pattern just as in filename expansion. If the pattern matches a trailing portion of the expanded value of *parameter*, then the result of the expansion is the value of *parameter* with the shortest matching pattern (the '%' case) or the longest matching pattern (the '%%' case) deleted. If *parameter* is '@' or '*', the pattern removal operation is applied to each positional parameter in turn, and the expansion is the resultant list. If *parameter*

is an array variable subscripted with '@' or '*', the pattern
removal operation is applied to each member of the array in
turn, and the expansion is the resultant list.

${*parameter*/*pattern*/*string*}

The *pattern* is expanded to produce a pattern just as in
filename expansion. *Parameter* is expanded and the longest
match of *pattern* against its value is replaced with *string*. If
pattern begins with '/', all matches of *pattern* are replaced
with *string*. Normally only the first match is replaced. If
pattern begins with '#', it must match at the beginning of
the expanded value of *parameter*. If *pattern* begins with '%',
it must match at the end of the expanded value of *parameter*.
If *string* is null, matches of *pattern* are deleted and the /
following *pattern* may be omitted. If *parameter* is '@' or
'*', the substitution operation is applied to each positional
parameter in turn, and the expansion is the resultant list.
If *parameter* is an array variable subscripted with '@' or '*',
the substitution operation is applied to each member of the
array in turn, and the expansion is the resultant list.

3.5.4 Command Substitution

Command substitution allows the output of a command to replace
the command itself. Command substitution occurs when a command is
enclosed as follows:

$(*command*)

or

`*command*`

Bash performs the expansion by executing *command* and replacing the
command substitution with the standard output of the command, with
any trailing newlines deleted. Embedded newlines are not deleted, but
they may be removed during word splitting. The command substitution
$(cat *file*) can be replaced by the equivalent but faster $(< *file*).

When the old-style backquote form of substitution is used, backslash
retains its literal meaning except when followed by '$', '`', or '\'. The
first backquote not preceded by a backslash terminates the command substitution. When using the $(*command*) form, all characters between the
parentheses make up the command; none are treated specially.

Command substitutions may be nested. To nest when using the back-
quoted form, escape the inner backquotes with backslashes.

If the substitution appears within double quotes, word splitting and
filename expansion are not performed on the results.

3.5.5 Arithmetic Expansion

Arithmetic expansion allows the evaluation of an arithmetic expression and the substitution of the result. The format for arithmetic expansion is:

$((*expression*))

The expression is treated as if it were within double quotes, but a double quote inside the parentheses is not treated specially. All tokens in the expression undergo parameter expansion, command substitution, and quote removal. Arithmetic expansions may be nested.

The evaluation is performed according to the rules listed below (see Section 6.5 [Shell Arithmetic], page 94). If the expression is invalid, Bash prints a message indicating failure to the standard error and no substitution occurs.

3.5.6 Process Substitution

Process substitution is supported on systems that support named pipes (FIFOs) or the '/dev/fd' method of naming open files. It takes the form of

<(*list*)

or

>(*list*)

The process *list* is run with its input or output connected to a FIFO or some file in '/dev/fd'. The name of this file is passed as an argument to the current command as the result of the expansion. If the >(*list*) form is used, writing to the file will provide input for *list*. If the <(*list*) form is used, the file passed as an argument should be read to obtain the output of *list*. Note that no space may appear between the < or > and the left parenthesis, otherwise the construct would be interpreted as a redirection.

When available, process substitution is performed simultaneously with parameter and variable expansion, command substitution, and arithmetic expansion.

3.5.7 Word Splitting

The shell scans the results of parameter expansion, command substitution, and arithmetic expansion that did not occur within double quotes for word splitting.

The shell treats each character of $IFS as a delimiter, and splits the results of the other expansions into words on these characters. If IFS is unset, or its value is exactly <space><tab><newline>, the default, then any sequence of IFS characters serves to delimit words. If IFS has a value other than the default, then sequences of the whitespace characters space and tab are ignored at the beginning and end of the word, as long as the whitespace character is in the value of IFS (an IFS whitespace character). Any character in IFS that is not IFS whitespace, along with any adjacent IFS whitespace characters, delimits a field. A sequence of IFS whitespace characters is also treated as a delimiter. If the value of IFS is null, no word splitting occurs.

Explicit null arguments ("" or '') are retained. Unquoted implicit null arguments, resulting from the expansion of parameters that have no values, are removed. If a parameter with no value is expanded within double quotes, a null argument results and is retained.

Note that if no expansion occurs, no splitting is performed.

3.5.8 Filename Expansion

After word splitting, unless the '-f' option has been set (see Section 4.3 [The Set Builtin], page 66), Bash scans each word for the characters '*', '?', and '['. If one of these characters appears, then the word is regarded as a *pattern*, and replaced with an alphabetically sorted list of file names matching the pattern. If no matching file names are found, and the shell option nullglob is disabled, the word is left unchanged. If the nullglob option is set, and no matches are found, the word is removed. If the failglob shell option is set, and no matches are found, an error message is printed and the command is not executed. If the shell option nocaseglob is enabled, the match is performed without regard to the case of alphabetic characters.

When a pattern is used for filename generation, the character '.' at the start of a filename or immediately following a slash must be matched explicitly, unless the shell option dotglob is set. When matching a file name, the slash character must always be matched explicitly. In other cases, the '.' character is not treated specially.

See the description of shopt in Section 4.2 [Bash Builtins], page 51, for a description of the nocaseglob, nullglob, failglob, and dotglob options.

The GLOBIGNORE shell variable may be used to restrict the set of file-names matching a pattern. If GLOBIGNORE is set, each matching filename that also matches one of the patterns in GLOBIGNORE is removed from the list of matches. The filenames '.' and '..' are always ignored when GLOBIGNORE is set and not null. However, setting GLOBIGNORE to a non-null value has the effect of enabling the dotglob shell option, so all other filenames beginning with a '.' will match. To get the old behavior of

ignoring filenames beginning with a '.', make '.*' one of the patterns in
GLOBIGNORE. The dotglob option is disabled when GLOBIGNORE is unset.

3.5.8.1 Pattern Matching

Any character that appears in a pattern, other than the special pattern
characters described below, matches itself. The NUL character may not
occur in a pattern. A backslash escapes the following character; the escaping backslash is discarded when matching. The special pattern characters
must be quoted if they are to be matched literally.

The special pattern characters have the following meanings:

*   Matches any string, including the null string.

?   Matches any single character.

[...]   Matches any one of the enclosed characters. A pair of char-
            acters separated by a hyphen denotes a *range expression*; any
            character that sorts between those two characters, inclusive,
            using the current locale's collating sequence and character
            set, is matched. If the first character following the '[' is a '!'
            or a '^' then any character not enclosed is matched. A '−'
            may be matched by including it as the first or last character
            in the set. A ']' may be matched by including it as the first
            character in the set. The sorting order of characters in range
            expressions is determined by the current locale and the value
            of the LC_COLLATE shell variable, if set.

            For example, in the default C locale, '[a−dx−z]' is equiv-
            alent to '[abcdxyz]'. Many locales sort characters in dic-
            tionary order, and in these locales '[a−dx−z]' is typically
            not equivalent to '[abcdxyz]'; it might be equivalent to
            '[aBbCcDdxXyYz]', for example. To obtain the traditional
            interpretation of ranges in bracket expressions, you can force
            the use of the C locale by setting the LC_COLLATE or LC_ALL
            environment variable to the value 'C'.

            Within '[' and ']', *character classes* can be specified using
            the syntax [:*class*:], where *class* is one of the following
            classes defined in the POSIX standard:

            alnum   alpha   ascii   blank   cntrl   digit
            graph   lower   print   punct   space   upper
            word   xdigit

            A character class matches any character belonging to that
            class. The word character class matches letters, digits, and
            the character '_'.

Within '[' and ']', an *equivalence class* can be specified using the syntax [=*c*=], which matches all characters with the
same collation weight (as defined by the current locale) as
the character *c*.

Within '[' and ']', the syntax [.*symbol*.] matches the collating symbol *symbol*.

If the extglob shell option is enabled using the shopt builtin, several
extended pattern matching operators are recognized. In the following
description, a *pattern-list* is a list of one or more patterns separated by a
'|'. Composite patterns may be formed using one or more of the following
sub-patterns:

?(*pattern-list*)
> Matches zero or one occurrence of the given patterns.

*(*pattern-list*)
> Matches zero or more occurrences of the given patterns.

+(*pattern-list*)
> Matches one or more occurrences of the given patterns.

@(*pattern-list*)
> Matches one of the given patterns.

!(*pattern-list*)
> Matches anything except one of the given patterns.

3.5.9 Quote Removal

After the preceding expansions, all unquoted occurrences of the characters '\', ' ' ', and '"' that did not result from one of the above expansions
are removed.

3.6 Redirections

Before a command is executed, its input and output may be *redirected* using a special notation interpreted by the shell. Redirection may
also be used to open and close files for the current shell execution environment. The following redirection operators may precede or appear
anywhere within a simple command or may follow a command. Redirections are processed in the order they appear, from left to right.

In the following descriptions, if the file descriptor number is omitted,
and the first character of the redirection operator is '<', the redirection
refers to the standard input (file descriptor 0). If the first character of the

redirection operator is '>', the redirection refers to the standard output (file descriptor 1).

The word following the redirection operator in the following descriptions, unless otherwise noted, is subjected to brace expansion, tilde expansion, parameter expansion, command substitution, arithmetic expansion, quote removal, filename expansion, and word splitting. If it expands to more than one word, Bash reports an error.

Note that the order of redirections is significant. For example, the command

> ls > *dirlist* 2>&1

directs both standard output (file descriptor 1) and standard error (file descriptor 2) to the file *dirlist*, while the command

> ls 2>&1 > *dirlist*

directs only the standard output to file *dirlist*, because the standard error was duplicated as standard output before the standard output was redirected to *dirlist*.

Bash handles several filenames specially when they are used in redirections, as described in the following table:

/dev/fd/*fd*
> If *fd* is a valid integer, file descriptor *fd* is duplicated.

/dev/stdin
> File descriptor 0 is duplicated.

/dev/stdout
> File descriptor 1 is duplicated.

/dev/stderr
> File descriptor 2 is duplicated.

/dev/tcp/*host*/*port*
> If *host* is a valid hostname or Internet address, and *port* is an integer port number or service name, Bash attempts to open a TCP connection to the corresponding socket.

/dev/udp/*host*/*port*
> If *host* is a valid hostname or Internet address, and *port* is an integer port number or service name, Bash attempts to open a UDP connection to the corresponding socket.

A failure to open or create a file causes the redirection to fail.

Redirections using file descriptors greater than 9 should be used with care, as they may conflict with file descriptors the shell uses internally.

3.6.1 Redirecting Input

Redirection of input causes the file whose name results from the expansion of *word* to be opened for reading on file descriptor n, or the standard input (file descriptor 0) if n is not specified.

The general format for redirecting input is:

    [n]<*word*

3.6.2 Redirecting Output

Redirection of output causes the file whose name results from the expansion of *word* to be opened for writing on file descriptor *n*, or the standard output (file descriptor 1) if *n* is not specified. If the file does not exist it is created; if it does exist it is truncated to zero size.

The general format for redirecting output is:

    [n]>[|]*word*

If the redirection operator is '>', and the noclobber option to the set builtin has been enabled, the redirection will fail if the file whose name results from the expansion of *word* exists and is a regular file. If the redirection operator is '>|', or the redirection operator is '>' and the noclobber option is not enabled, the redirection is attempted even if the file named by *word* exists.

3.6.3 Appending Redirected Output

Redirection of output in this fashion causes the file whose name results from the expansion of *word* to be opened for appending on file descriptor *n*, or the standard output (file descriptor 1) if *n* is not specified. If the file does not exist it is created.

The general format for appending output is:

    [n]>>*word*

3.6.4 Redirecting Standard Output and Standard Error

Bash allows both the standard output (file descriptor 1) and the standard error output (file descriptor 2) to be redirected to the file whose name is the expansion of *word* with this construct.

There are two formats for redirecting standard output and standard error:

    &>*word*

and

>&*word*

Of the two forms, the first is preferred. This is semantically equivalent to

>*word* 2>&1

3.6.5 Here Documents

This type of redirection instructs the shell to read input from the current source until a line containing only *word* (with no trailing blanks) is seen. All of the lines read up to that point are then used as the standard input for a command.

The format of here-documents is:

<<[−] *word*
        here-document
delimiter

No parameter expansion, command substitution, arithmetic expansion, or filename expansion is performed on *word*. If any characters in *word* are quoted, the *delimiter* is the result of quote removal on *word*, and the lines in the here-document are not expanded. If *word* is unquoted, all lines of the here-document are subjected to parameter expansion, command substitution, and arithmetic expansion. In the latter case, the character sequence \newline is ignored, and '\' must be used to quote the characters '\', '$', and '`'.

If the redirection operator is '<<−', then all leading tab characters are stripped from input lines and the line containing *delimiter*. This allows here-documents within shell scripts to be indented in a natural fashion.

3.6.6 Here Strings

A variant of here documents, the format is:

<<< *word*

The *word* is expanded and supplied to the command on its standard input.

3.6.7 Duplicating File Descriptors

The redirection operator

[*n*]<&*word*

is used to duplicate input file descriptors. If *word* expands to one or more digits, the file descriptor denoted by *n* is made to be a copy of that file descriptor. If the digits in *word* do not specify a file descriptor open for input, a redirection error occurs. If *word* evaluates to '−', file descriptor *n* is closed. If *n* is not specified, the standard input (file descriptor 0) is used.

The operator

    [*n*] >&*word*

is used similarly to duplicate output file descriptors. If *n* is not specified, the standard output (file descriptor 1) is used. If the digits in *word* do not specify a file descriptor open for output, a redirection error occurs. As a special case, if *n* is omitted, and *word* does not expand to one or more digits, the standard output and standard error are redirected as described previously.

3.6.8 Moving File Descriptors

The redirection operator

    [*n*] <&*digit-*

moves the file descriptor *digit* to file descriptor *n*, or the standard input (file descriptor 0) if *n* is not specified. *digit* is closed after being duplicated to *n*.

Similarly, the redirection operator

    [*n*] >&*digit-*

moves the file descriptor *digit* to file descriptor *n*, or the standard output (file descriptor 1) if *n* is not specified.

3.6.9 Opening File Descriptors for Reading and Writing

The redirection operator

    [*n*] <>*word*

causes the file whose name is the expansion of *word* to be opened for both reading and writing on file descriptor *n*, or on file descriptor 0 if *n* is not specified. If the file does not exist, it is created.

3.7 Executing Commands

3.7.1 Simple Command Expansion

When a simple command is executed, the shell performs the following expansions, assignments, and redirections, from left to right.

1. The words that the parser has marked as variable assignments (those preceding the command name) and redirections are saved for later processing.

2. The words that are not variable assignments or redirections are expanded (see Section 3.5 [Shell Expansions], page 22). If any words remain after expansion, the first word is taken to be the name of the command and the remaining words are the arguments.

3. Redirections are performed as described above (see Section 3.6 [Redirections], page 32).

4. The text after the '=' in each variable assignment undergoes tilde expansion, parameter expansion, command substitution, arithmetic expansion, and quote removal before being assigned to the variable.

If no command name results, the variable assignments affect the current shell environment. Otherwise, the variables are added to the environment of the executed command and do not affect the current shell environment. If any of the assignments attempts to assign a value to a readonly variable, an error occurs, and the command exits with a non-zero status.

If no command name results, redirections are performed, but do not affect the current shell environment. A redirection error causes the command to exit with a non-zero status.

If there is a command name left after expansion, execution proceeds as described below. Otherwise, the command exits. If one of the expansions contained a command substitution, the exit status of the command is the exit status of the last command substitution performed. If there were no command substitutions, the command exits with a status of zero.

3.7.2 Command Search and Execution

After a command has been split into words, if it results in a simple command and an optional list of arguments, the following actions are taken.

1. If the command name contains no slashes, the shell attempts to locate it. If there exists a shell function by that name, that function is invoked as described in Section 3.3 [Shell Functions], page 18.

2. If the name does not match a function, the shell searches for it in the list of shell builtins. If a match is found, that builtin is invoked.

3. If the name is neither a shell function nor a builtin, and contains no slashes, Bash searches each element of $PATH for a directory containing an executable file by that name. Bash uses a hash table to remember the full pathnames of executable files to avoid multiple PATH searches (see the description of hash in Section 4.1 [Bourne Shell Builtins], page 43). A full search of the directories in $PATH is performed only if the command is not found in the hash table. If the

search is unsuccessful, the shell prints an error message and returns an exit status of 127.

4. If the search is successful, or if the command name contains one or more slashes, the shell executes the named program in a separate execution environment. Argument 0 is set to the name given, and the remaining arguments to the command are set to the arguments supplied, if any.

5. If this execution fails because the file is not in executable format, and the file is not a directory, it is assumed to be a *shell script* and the shell executes it as described in Section 3.8 [Shell Scripts], page 41.

6. If the command was not begun asynchronously, the shell waits for the command to complete and collects its exit status.

3.7.3 Command Execution Environment

The shell has an *execution environment*, which consists of the following:

- open files inherited by the shell at invocation, as modified by redirections supplied to the exec builtin
- the current working directory as set by cd, pushd, or popd, or inherited by the shell at invocation
- the file creation mode mask as set by umask or inherited from the shell's parent
- current traps set by trap
- shell parameters that are set by variable assignment or with set or inherited from the shell's parent in the environment
- shell functions defined during execution or inherited from the shell's parent in the environment
- options enabled at invocation (either by default or with command-line arguments) or by set
- options enabled by shopt
- shell aliases defined with alias (see Section 6.6 [Aliases], page 95)
- various process IDs, including those of background jobs (see Section 3.2.3 [Lists], page 12), the value of $$, and the value of $PPID

When a simple command other than a builtin or shell function is to be executed, it is invoked in a separate execution environment that consists of the following. Unless otherwise noted, the values are inherited from the shell.

- the shell's open files, plus any modifications and additions specified by redirections to the command

- the current working directory

- the file creation mode mask

- shell variables and functions marked for export, along with variables exported for the command, passed in the environment (see Section 3.7.4 [Environment], page 39)

- traps caught by the shell are reset to the values inherited from the shell's parent, and traps ignored by the shell are ignored

A command invoked in this separate environment cannot affect the shell's execution environment.

Command substitution, commands grouped with parentheses, and asynchronous commands are invoked in a subshell environment that is a duplicate of the shell environment, except that traps caught by the shell are reset to the values that the shell inherited from its parent at invocation. Builtin commands that are invoked as part of a pipeline are also executed in a subshell environment. Changes made to the subshell environment cannot affect the shell's execution environment.

If a command is followed by an ampersand '&' and job control is not active, the default standard input for the command is the empty file '/dev/null'. Otherwise, the invoked command inherits the file descriptors of the calling shell as modified by redirections.

3.7.4 Environment

When a program is invoked it is given an array of strings called the *environment*. This is a list of name-value pairs, of the form name=value.

Bash provides several ways to manipulate the environment. On invocation, the shell scans its own environment and creates a parameter for each name found, automatically marking it for *export* to child processes. Executed commands inherit the environment. The export and 'declare -x' commands allow parameters and functions to be added to and deleted from the environment. If the value of a parameter in the environment is modified, the new value becomes part of the environment, replacing the old. The environment inherited by any executed command consists of the shell's initial environment, whose values may be modified in the shell, less any pairs removed by the unset and 'export -n' commands, plus any additions via the export and 'declare -x' commands.

The environment for any simple command or function may be augmented temporarily by prefixing it with parameter assignments, as described in Section 3.4 [Shell Parameters], page 20. These assignment statements affect only the environment seen by that command.

If the '-k' option is set (see Section 4.3 [The Set Builtin], page 66), then all parameter assignments are placed in the environment for a command, not just those that precede the command name.

When Bash invokes an external command, the variable '$_' is set to the full path name of the command and passed to that command in its environment.

3.7.5 Exit Status

For the shell's purposes, a command which exits with a zero exit status has succeeded. A non-zero exit status indicates failure. This seemingly counter-intuitive scheme is used so there is one well-defined way to indicate success and a variety of ways to indicate various failure modes. When a command terminates on a fatal signal whose number is N, Bash uses the value 128+N as the exit status.

If a command is not found, the child process created to execute it returns a status of 127. If a command is found but is not executable, the return status is 126.

If a command fails because of an error during expansion or redirection, the exit status is greater than zero.

The exit status is used by the Bash conditional commands (see Section 3.2.4.2 [Conditional Constructs], page 14) and some of the list constructs (see Section 3.2.3 [Lists], page 12).

All of the Bash builtins return an exit status of zero if they succeed and a non-zero status on failure, so they may be used by the conditional and list constructs. All builtins return an exit status of 2 to indicate incorrect usage.

3.7.6 Signals

When Bash is interactive, in the absence of any traps, it ignores SIGTERM (so that 'kill 0' does not kill an interactive shell), and SIGINT is caught and handled (so that the wait builtin is interruptible). When Bash receives a SIGINT, it breaks out of any executing loops. In all cases, Bash ignores SIGQUIT. If job control is in effect (see Chapter 7 [Job Control], page 107), Bash ignores SIGTTIN, SIGTTOU, and SIGTSTP.

Non-builtin commands started by Bash have signal handlers set to the values inherited by the shell from its parent. When job control is not in effect, asynchronous commands ignore SIGINT and SIGQUIT in addition to these inherited handlers. Commands run as a result of command substitution ignore the keyboard-generated job control signals SIGTTIN, SIGTTOU, and SIGTSTP.

The shell exits by default upon receipt of a SIGHUP. Before exiting, an interactive shell resends the SIGHUP to all jobs, running or stopped. Stopped jobs are sent SIGCONT to ensure that they receive the SIGHUP. To prevent the shell from sending the SIGHUP signal to a particular job, it should be removed from the jobs table with the disown builtin (see Section 7.2 [Job Control Builtins], page 108) or marked to not receive SIGHUP using disown -h.

If the huponexit shell option has been set with shopt (see Section 4.2 [Bash Builtins], page 51), Bash sends a SIGHUP to all jobs when an interactive login shell exits.

If Bash is waiting for a command to complete and receives a signal for which a trap has been set, the trap will not be executed until the command completes. When Bash is waiting for an asynchronous command via the wait builtin, the reception of a signal for which a trap has been set will cause the wait builtin to return immediately with an exit status greater than 128, immediately after which the trap is executed.

3.8 Shell Scripts

A shell script is a text file containing shell commands. When such a file is used as the first non-option argument when invoking Bash, and neither the '-c' nor '-s' option is supplied (see Section 6.1 [Invoking Bash], page 85), Bash reads and executes commands from the file, then exits. This mode of operation creates a non-interactive shell. The shell first searches for the file in the current directory, and looks in the directories in $PATH if not found there.

When Bash runs a shell script, it sets the special parameter 0 to the name of the file, rather than the name of the shell, and the positional parameters are set to the remaining arguments, if any are given. If no additional arguments are supplied, the positional parameters are unset.

A shell script may be made executable by using the chmod command to turn on the execute bit. When Bash finds such a file while searching the $PATH for a command, it spawns a subshell to execute it. In other words, executing

    filename *arguments*

is equivalent to executing

    bash filename *arguments*

if filename is an executable shell script. This subshell reinitializes itself, so that the effect is as if a new shell had been invoked to interpret the script, with the exception that the locations of commands remembered by the parent (see the description of hash in Section 4.1 [Bourne Shell Builtins], page 43) are retained by the child.

Most versions of Unix make this a part of the operating system's command execution mechanism. If the first line of a script begins with the two characters '#!', the remainder of the line specifies an interpreter for the program. Thus, you can specify Bash, awk, Perl, or some other interpreter and write the rest of the script file in that language.

The arguments to the interpreter consist of a single optional argument following the interpreter name on the first line of the script file, followed by the name of the script file, followed by the rest of the arguments. Bash will perform this action on operating systems that do not handle it themselves. Note that some older versions of Unix limit the interpreter name and argument to a maximum of 32 characters.

Bash scripts often begin with #! /bin/bash (assuming that Bash has been installed in '/bin'), since this ensures that Bash will be used to interpret the script, even if it is executed under another shell.

4 Shell Builtin Commands

Builtin commands are contained within the shell itself. When the name of a builtin command is used as the first word of a simple command (see Section 3.2.1 [Simple Commands], page 10), the shell executes the command directly, without invoking another program. Builtin commands are necessary to implement functionality impossible or inconvenient to obtain with separate utilities.

This section briefly describes the builtins which Bash inherits from the Bourne Shell, as well as the builtin commands which are unique to or have been extended in Bash.

Several builtin commands are described in other chapters: builtin commands which provide the Bash interface to the job control facilities (see Section 7.2 [Job Control Builtins], page 108), the directory stack (see Section 6.8.1 [Directory Stack Builtins], page 98), the command history (see Section 9.2 [Bash History Builtins], page 146), and the programmable completion facilities (see Section 8.7 [Programmable Completion Builtins], page 141).

Many of the builtins have been extended by POSIX or Bash.

Unless otherwise noted, each builtin command documented as accepting options preceded by '-' accepts '--' to signify the end of the options. For example, the :, true, false, and test builtins do not accept options.

4.1 Bourne Shell Builtins

The following shell builtin commands are inherited from the Bourne Shell. These commands are implemented as specified by the POSIX standard.

: (a colon)

> : [arguments]
>
> Do nothing beyond expanding arguments and performing redirections. The return status is zero.

. (a period)

> . filename [arguments]
>
> Read and execute commands from the filename argument in the current shell context. If filename does not contain a slash, the PATH variable is used to find filename. When Bash is not in POSIX mode, the current directory is searched if filename is not found in $PATH. If any arguments are supplied,

they become the positional parameters when *filename* is executed. Otherwise the positional parameters are unchanged. The return status is the exit status of the last command executed, or zero if no commands are executed. If *filename* is not found, or cannot be read, the return status is non-zero. This builtin is equivalent to source.

break

> `break [n]`
>
> Exit from a for, while, until, or select loop. If *n* is supplied, the *n*th enclosing loop is exited. *n* must be greater than or equal to 1. The return status is zero unless *n* is not greater than or equal to 1.

cd

> `cd [-L|-P] [directory]`
>
> Change the current working directory to *directory*. If *directory* is not given, the value of the HOME shell variable is used. If the shell variable CDPATH exists, it is used as a search path. If *directory* begins with a slash, CDPATH is not used.
>
> The '-P' option means to not follow symbolic links; symbolic links are followed by default or with the '-L' option. If *directory* is '-', it is equivalent to $OLDPWD.
>
> If a non-empty directory name from CDPATH is used, or if '-' is the first argument, and the directory change is successful, the absolute pathname of the new working directory is written to the standard output.
>
> The return status is zero if the directory is successfully changed, non-zero otherwise.

continue

> `continue [n]`
>
> Resume the next iteration of an enclosing for, while, until, or select loop. If *n* is supplied, the execution of the *n*th enclosing loop is resumed. *n* must be greater than or equal to 1. The return status is zero unless *n* is not greater than or equal to 1.

eval

> `eval [arguments]`
>
> The arguments are concatenated together into a single command, which is then read and executed, and its exit status returned as the exit status of eval. If there are no arguments or only empty arguments, the return status is zero.

exec

> exec [-cl] [-a *name*] [*command* [*arguments*]]
>
> If *command* is supplied, it replaces the shell without creat-
> ing a new process. If the '-l' option is supplied, the shell
> places a dash at the beginning of the zeroth argument passed
> to *command*. This is what the login program does. The
> '-c' option causes *command* to be executed with an empty
> environment. If '-a' is supplied, the shell passes *name* as the
> zeroth argument to *command*. If no *command* is specified,
> redirections may be used to affect the current shell environ-
> ment. If there are no redirection errors, the return status is
> zero; otherwise the return status is non-zero.

exit

> exit [*n*]
>
> Exit the shell, returning a status of *n* to the shell's parent.
> If *n* is omitted, the exit status is that of the last command
> executed. Any trap on EXIT is executed before the shell
> terminates.

export

> export [-fn] [-p] [*name*[=*value*]]
>
> Mark each *name* to be passed to child processes in the en-
> vironment. If the '-f' option is supplied, the *names* refer
> to shell functions; otherwise the names refer to shell vari-
> ables. The '-n' option means to no longer mark each *name*
> for export. If no *names* are supplied, or if the '-p' option is
> given, a list of exported names is displayed. The '-p' option
> displays output in a form that may be reused as input. If a
> variable name is followed by =*value*, the value of the variable
> is set to *value*.
>
> The return status is zero unless an invalid option is supplied,
> one of the names is not a valid shell variable name, or '-f'
> is supplied with a name that is not a shell function.

getopts

> getopts *optstring* *name* [*args*]
>
> getopts is used by shell scripts to parse positional param-
> eters. *optstring* contains the option characters to be rec-
> ognized; if a character is followed by a colon, the option is
> expected to have an argument, which should be separated
> from it by white space. The colon (':') and question mark
> ('?') may not be used as option characters. Each time it is

invoked, getopts places the next option in the shell variable *name*, initializing *name* if it does not exist, and the index of the next argument to be processed into the variable OPTIND. OPTIND is initialized to 1 each time the shell or a shell script is invoked. When an option requires an argument, getopts places that argument into the variable OPTARG. The shell does not reset OPTIND automatically; it must be manually reset between multiple calls to getopts within the same shell invocation if a new set of parameters is to be used.

When the end of options is encountered, getopts exits with a return value greater than zero. OPTIND is set to the index of the first non-option argument, and name is set to '?'.

getopts normally parses the positional parameters, but if more arguments are given in *args*, getopts parses those instead.

getopts can report errors in two ways. If the first character of *optstring* is a colon, *silent* error reporting is used. In normal operation diagnostic messages are printed when invalid options or missing option arguments are encountered. If the variable OPTERR is set to 0, no error messages will be displayed, even if the first character of optstring is not a colon.

If an invalid option is seen, getopts places '?' into *name* and, if not silent, prints an error message and unsets OPTARG. If getopts is silent, the option character found is placed in OPTARG and no diagnostic message is printed.

If a required argument is not found, and getopts is not silent, a question mark ('?') is placed in *name*, OPTARG is unset, and a diagnostic message is printed. If getopts is silent, then a colon (':') is placed in *name* and OPTARG is set to the option character found.

hash

    hash [-r] [-p *filename*] [-dt] [*name*]

Remember the full pathnames of commands specified as *name* arguments, so they need not be searched for on subsequent invocations. The commands are found by searching through the directories listed in $PATH. The '-p' option inhibits the path search, and *filename* is used as the location of *name*. The '-r' option causes the shell to forget all remembered locations. The '-d' option causes the shell to forget

the remembered location of each *name*. If the '-t' option is
supplied, the full pathname to which each *name* corresponds
is printed. If multiple *name* arguments are supplied with '-t'
the *name* is printed before the hashed full pathname. The
'-l' option causes output to be displayed in a format that
may be reused as input. If no arguments are given, or if only
'-l' is supplied, information about remembered commands
is printed. The return status is zero unless a *name* is not
found or an invalid option is supplied.

pwd

pwd [-LP]

Print the absolute pathname of the current working directory. If the '-P' option is supplied, the pathname printed will
not contain symbolic links. If the '-L' option is supplied, the
pathname printed may contain symbolic links. The return
status is zero unless an error is encountered while determin-
ing the name of the current directory or an invalid option is
supplied.

readonly

readonly [-apf] [*name*[=*value*]] ...

Mark each *name* as readonly. The values of these names may
not be changed by subsequent assignment. If the '-f' option
is supplied, each *name* refers to a shell function. The '-a'
option means each *name* refers to an array variable. If no
name arguments are given, or if the '-p' option is supplied, a
list of all readonly names is printed. The '-p' option causes
output to be displayed in a format that may be reused as
input. If a variable name is followed by =*value*, the value of
the variable is set to *value*. The return status is zero unless
an invalid option is supplied, one of the *name* arguments is
not a valid shell variable or function name, or the '-f' option
is supplied with a name that is not a shell function.

return

return [*n*]

Cause a shell function to exit with the return value *n*. If *n*
is not supplied, the return value is the exit status of the last
command executed in the function. This may also be used to
terminate execution of a script being executed with the . (or
source) builtin, returning either *n* or the exit status of the
last command executed within the script as the exit status
of the script. Any command associated with the RETURN

trap is executed before execution resumes after the function or script. The return status is non-zero if `return` is used outside a function and not during the execution of a script by . or `source`.

shift

> shift [n]

> Shift the positional parameters to the left by n. The positional parameters from n+1 ... $# are renamed to $1 ... $#-n+1. Parameters represented by the numbers $# to n+1 are unset. n must be a non-negative number less than or equal to $#. If n is zero or greater than $#, the positional parameters are not changed. If n is not supplied, it is assumed to be 1. The return status is zero unless n is greater than $# or less than zero, non-zero otherwise.

test
[

> Evaluate a conditional expression expr. Each operator and operand must be a separate argument. Expressions are composed of the primaries described below in Section 6.4 [Bash Conditional Expressions], page 92. test does not accept any options, nor does it accept and ignore an argument of '--' as signifying the end of options.

> When the [form is used, the last argument to the command must be a].

> Expressions may be combined using the following operators, listed in decreasing order of precedence.

> ! expr   True if expr is false.

> (expr)   Returns the value of expr. This may be used to override the normal precedence of operators.

> expr1 -a expr2
> > True if both expr1 and expr2 are true.

> expr1 -o expr2
> > True if either expr1 or expr2 is true.

> The test and [builtins evaluate conditional expressions using a set of rules based on the number of arguments.

> 0 arguments
> > The expression is false.

> 1 argument The expression is true if and only if the argument is not null.

2 arguments

If the first argument is '!', the expression is true if and only if the second argument is null. If the first argument is one of the unary conditional operators (see Section 6.4 [Bash Conditional Expressions], page 92), the expression is true if the unary test is true. If the first argument is not a valid unary operator, the expression is false.

3 arguments

If the second argument is one of the binary conditional operators (see Section 6.4 [Bash Conditional Expressions], page 92), the result of the expression is the result of the binary test using the first and third arguments as operands. If the first argument is '!', the value is the negation of the two-argument test using the second and third arguments. If the first argument is exactly '(' and the third argument is exactly ')', the result is the one-argument test of the second argument. Otherwise, the expression is false. The '-a' and '-o' operators are considered binary operators in this case.

4 arguments

If the first argument is '!', the result is the negation of the three-argument expression composed of the remaining arguments. Otherwise, the expression is parsed and evaluated according to precedence using the rules listed above.

5 or more arguments

The expression is parsed and evaluated according to precedence using the rules listed above.

times

times

Print out the user and system times used by the shell and its children. The return status is zero.

trap

trap [-lp] [arg] [sigspec ...]

The commands in arg are to be read and executed when the shell receives signal sigspec. If arg is absent (and there is a

single *sigspec*) or equal to '-', each specified signal's disposition is reset to the value it had when the shell was started.
If *arg* is the null string, then the signal specified by each
sigspec is ignored by the shell and commands it invokes. If
arg is not present and '-p' has been supplied, the shell displays the trap commands associated with each *sigspec*. If
no arguments are supplied, or only '-p' is given, trap prints
the list of commands associated with each signal number in
a form that may be reused as shell input. The '-l' option
causes the shell to print a list of signal names and their corresponding numbers. Each *sigspec* is either a signal name
or a signal number. Signal names are case insensitive and
the SIG prefix is optional. If a *sigspec* is 0 or EXIT, *arg*
is executed when the shell exits. If a *sigspec* is DEBUG, the
command *arg* is executed before every simple command, for
command, case command, select command, every arithmetic for command, and before the first command executes
in a shell function. Refer to the description of the extglob
option to the shopt builtin (see Section 4.2 [Bash Builtins],
page 51) for details of its effect on the DEBUG trap. If a
sigspec is ERR, the command *arg* is executed whenever a
simple command has a non-zero exit status, subject to the
following conditions. The ERR trap is not executed if the
failed command is part of the command list immediately following an until or while keyword, part of the test in an if
statement, part of a && or || list, or if the command's return
status is being inverted using !. These are the same conditions obeyed by the errexit option. If a *sigspec* is RETURN,
the command *arg* is executed each time a shell function or
a script executed with the . or source builtins finishes executing.

Signals ignored upon entry to the shell cannot be trapped or
reset. Trapped signals that are not being ignored are reset
to their original values in a child process when it is created.

The return status is zero unless a *sigspec* does not specify a
valid signal.

umask

umask [-p] [-S] [*mode*]

Set the shell process's file creation mask to *mode*. If *mode*
begins with a digit, it is interpreted as an octal number; if
not, it is interpreted as a symbolic mode mask similar to
that accepted by the chmod command. If *mode* is omitted,

the current value of the mask is printed. If the '-S' option is supplied without a *mode* argument, the mask is printed in a symbolic format. If the '-p' option is supplied, and *mode* is omitted, the output is in a form that may be reused as input. The return status is zero if the mode is successfully changed or if no *mode* argument is supplied, and non-zero otherwise.

Note that when the mode is interpreted as an octal number, each number of the umask is subtracted from 7. Thus, a umask of 022 results in permissions of 755.

unset

> unset [-fv] [*name*]

Each variable or function *name* is removed. If no options are supplied, or the '-v' option is given, each *name* refers to a shell variable. If the '-f' option is given, the *names* refer to shell functions, and the function definition is removed. Readonly variables and functions may not be unset. The return status is zero unless a *name* is readonly.

4.2 Bash Builtin Commands

This section describes builtin commands which are unique to or have been extended in Bash. Some of these commands are specified in the POSIX standard.

alias

> alias [-p] [*name*[=*value*] ...]

Without arguments or with the '-p' option, alias prints the list of aliases on the standard output in a form that allows them to be reused as input. If arguments are supplied, an alias is defined for each *name* whose *value* is given. If no *value* is given, the name and value of the alias is printed. Aliases are described in Section 6.6 [Aliases], page 95.

bind

> bind [-m *keymap*] [-lpsvPSV]
> bind [-m *keymap*] [-q *function*] [-u *function*]
>   [-r *keyseq*]
> bind [-m *keymap*] -f *filename*
> bind [-m *keymap*] -x *keyseq:shell-command*
> bind [-m *keymap*] *keyseq:function-name*
> bind *readline-command*

Display current Readline (see Chapter 8 [Command Line Editing], page 113) key and function bindings, bind a key sequence to a Readline function or macro, or set a Readline variable. Each non-option argument is a command as it would appear in a Readline initialization file (see Section 8.3 [Readline Init File], page 117), but each binding or command must be passed as a separate argument; e.g., '"\C-x\C-r":re-read-init-file'. Options, if supplied, have the following meanings:

-m *keymap*   Use *keymap* as the keymap to be affected by the subsequent bindings. Acceptable *keymap* names are emacs, emacs-standard, emacs-meta, emacs-ctlx, vi, vi-move, vi-command, and vi-insert. vi is equivalent to vi-command; emacs is equivalent to emacs-standard.

-l   List the names of all Readline functions.

-p   Display Readline function names and bindings in such a way that they can be used as input or in a Readline initialization file.

-P   List current Readline function names and bindings.

-v   Display Readline variable names and values in such a way that they can be used as input or in a Readline initialization file.

-V   List current Readline variable names and values.

-s   Display Readline key sequences bound to macros and the strings they output in such a way that they can be used as input or in a Readline initialization file.

-S   Display Readline key sequences bound to macros and the strings they output.

-f *filename*   Read key bindings from *filename*.

-q *function*   Query about which keys invoke the named *function*.

-u *function*   Unbind all keys bound to the named *function*.

-r *keyseq*   Remove any current binding for *keyseq*.

-x *keyseq:shell-command*

> Cause *shell-command* to be executed whenever *keyseq* is entered.

The return status is zero unless an invalid option is supplied or an error occurs.

builtin

> builtin [*shell-builtin* [*args*]]

Run a shell builtin, passing it *args*, and return its exit status. This is useful when defining a shell function with the same name as a shell builtin, retaining the functionality of the builtin within the function. The return status is non-zero if *shell-builtin* is not a shell builtin command.

caller

> caller [*expr*]

Returns the context of any active subroutine call (a shell function or a script executed with the . or source builtins).

Without *expr*, caller displays the line number and source filename of the current subroutine call. If a non-negative integer is supplied as *expr*, caller displays the line number, subroutine name, and source file corresponding to that position in the current execution call stack. This extra information may be used, for example, to print a stack trace. The current frame is frame 0.

The return value is 0 unless the shell is not executing a subroutine call or *expr* does not correspond to a valid position in the call stack.

command

> command [-pVv] *command* [*arguments* ...]

Runs *command* with *arguments* ignoring any shell function named *command*. Only shell builtin commands or commands found by searching the PATH are executed. If there is a shell function named ls, running 'command ls' within the function will execute the external command ls instead of calling the function recursively. The '-p' option means to use a default value for PATH that is guaranteed to find all of the standard utilities. The return status in this case is 127 if *command* cannot be found or an error occurred, and the exit status of *command* otherwise.

If either the '-V' or '-v' option is supplied, a description of *command* is printed. The '-v' option causes a single word indicating the command or file name used to invoke *command* to be displayed; the '-V' option produces a more verbose description. In this case, the return status is zero if *command* is found, and non-zero if not.

declare

> declare [-afFirtx] [-p] [*name*[=*value*] ...]

Declare variables and give them attributes. If no *names* are given, then display the values of variables instead.

The '-p' option will display the attributes and values of each *name*. When '-p' is used, additional options are ignored. The '-F' option inhibits the display of function definitions; only the function name and attributes are printed. If the extdebug shell option is enabled using shopt (see Section 4.2 [Bash Builtins], page 51), the source file name and line number where the function is defined are displayed as well. '-F' implies '-f'. The following options can be used to restrict output to variables with the specified attributes or to give variables attributes:

-a   Each *name* is an array variable (see Section 6.7 [Arrays], page 96).

-f   Use function names only.

-i   The variable is to be treated as an integer; arithmetic evaluation (see Section 6.5 [Shell Arithmetic], page 94) is performed when the variable is assigned a value.

-r   Make *names* readonly. These names cannot then be assigned values by subsequent assignment statements or unset.

-t   Give each *name* the trace attribute. Traced functions inherit the DEBUG and RETURN traps from the calling shell. The trace attribute has no special meaning for variables.

-x   Mark each *name* for export to subsequent commands via the environment.

Using '+' instead of '-' turns off the attribute instead. When used in a function, declare makes each *name* local, as with the local command. If a variable name is followed by =*value*, the value of the variable is set to *value*.

The return status is zero unless an invalid option is encountered, an attempt is made to define a function using '-f
foo=bar', an attempt is made to assign a value to a readonly variable, an attempt is made to assign a value to an
array variable without using the compound assignment syntax (see Section 6.7 [Arrays], page 96), one of the *names*
is not a valid shell variable name, an attempt is made to
turn off readonly status for a readonly variable, an attempt
is made to turn off array status for an array variable, or an
attempt is made to display a non-existent function with '-f'.

echo

echo [-neE] [*arg* ...]

Output the *args*, separated by spaces, terminated with a
newline. The return status is always 0. If '-n' is specified,
the trailing newline is suppressed. If the '-e' option is given,
interpretation of the following backslash-escaped characters
is enabled. The '-E' option disables the interpretation of
these escape characters, even on systems where they are interpreted by default. The xpg_echo shell option may be used
to dynamically determine whether or not echo expands these
escape characters by default. echo does not interpret '--' to
mean the end of options.

echo interprets the following escape sequences:

\a   alert (bell)

\b   backspace

\c   suppress trailing newline

\e   escape

\f   form feed

\n   new line

\r   carriage return

\t   horizontal tab

\v   vertical tab

\\   backslash

\0*nnn*   the eight-bit character whose value is the octal
            value *nnn* (zero to three octal digits)

\x*HH*   the eight-bit character whose value is the hex-
            adecimal value *HH* (one or two hex digits)

enable

> enable [-n] [-p] [-f *filename*] [-ads] [*name* ...]
>
> Enable and disable builtin shell commands. Disabling a builtin allows a disk command which has the same name as a shell builtin to be executed without specifying a full pathname, even though the shell normally searches for builtins before disk commands. If '-n' is used, the *names* become disabled. Otherwise *names* are enabled. For example, to use the test binary found via $PATH instead of the shell builtin version, type 'enable -n test'.
>
> If the '-p' option is supplied, or no *name* arguments appear, a list of shell builtins is printed. With no other arguments, the list consists of all enabled shell builtins. The '-a' option means to list each builtin with an indication of whether or not it is enabled.
>
> The '-f' option means to load the new builtin command *name* from shared object *filename*, on systems that support dynamic loading. The '-d' option will delete a builtin loaded with '-f'.
>
> If there are no options, a list of the shell builtins is displayed. The '-s' option restricts enable to the POSIX special builtins. If '-s' is used with '-f', the new builtin becomes a special builtin (see Section 4.4 [Special Builtins], page 70).
>
> The return status is zero unless a *name* is not a shell builtin or there is an error loading a new builtin from a shared object.

help

> help [-s] [*pattern*]
>
> Display helpful information about builtin commands. If *pattern* is specified, help gives detailed help on all commands matching *pattern*, otherwise a list of the builtins is printed. The '-s' option restricts the information displayed to a short usage synopsis. The return status is zero unless no command matches *pattern*.

let

> let *expression* [*expression*]
>
> The let builtin allows arithmetic to be performed on shell variables. Each *expression* is evaluated according to the rules given below in Section 6.5 [Shell Arithmetic], page 94. If the last *expression* evaluates to 0, let returns 1; otherwise 0 is returned.

local

> local [*option*] *name*[=*value*] ...

For each argument, a local variable named *name* is created, and assigned *value*. The *option* can be any of the options accepted by declare. local can only be used within a function; it makes the variable *name* have a visible scope restricted to that function and its children. The return status is zero unless local is used outside a function, an invalid *name* is supplied, or *name* is a readonly variable.

logout

> logout [*n*]

Exit a login shell, returning a status of *n* to the shell's parent.

printf

> printf [-v *var*] *format* [*arguments*]

Write the formatted *arguments* to the standard output under the control of the *format*. The *format* is a character string which contains three types of objects: plain characters, which are simply copied to standard output, character escape sequences, which are converted and copied to the standard output, and format specifications, each of which causes printing of the next successive *argument*. In addition to the standard printf(1) formats, '%b' causes printf to expand backslash escape sequences in the corresponding *argument*, (except that '\c' terminates output, backslashes in '\'', '\"', and '\?' are not removed, and octal escapes beginning with '\0' may contain up to four digits), and '%q' causes printf to output the corresponding *argument* in a format that can be reused as shell input.

The '-v' option causes the output to be assigned to the variable *var* rather than being printed to the standard output.

The *format* is reused as necessary to consume all of the *arguments*. If the *format* requires more *arguments* than are supplied, the extra format specifications behave as if a zero value or null string, as appropriate, had been supplied. The return value is zero on success, non-zero on failure.

read

> read [-ers] [-a *aname*] [-d *delim*] [-n *nchars*]
> [-p *prompt*] [-t *timeout*] [-u *fd*] [*name* ...]

One line is read from the standard input, or from the file descriptor *fd* supplied as an argument to the '-u' option,

and the first word is assigned to the first *name*, the second
word to the second *name*, and so on, with leftover words
and their intervening separators assigned to the last *name*.
If there are fewer words read from the input stream than
names, the remaining names are assigned empty values. The
characters in the value of the IFS variable are used to split
the line into words. The backslash character '\' may be used
to remove any special meaning for the next character read
and for line continuation. If no names are supplied, the line
read is assigned to the variable REPLY. The return code is
zero, unless end-of-file is encountered, read times out, or an
invalid file descriptor is supplied as the argument to '-u'.
Options, if supplied, have the following meanings:

-a *aname*   The words are assigned to sequential indices of
                the array variable *aname*, starting at 0. All el-
                ements are removed from *aname* before the as-
                signment. Other *name* arguments are ignored.

-d *delim*   The first character of *delim* is used to terminate
                the input line, rather than newline.

-e   Readline (see Chapter 8 [Command Line Edit-
                ing], page 113) is used to obtain the line.

-n *nchars*   read returns after reading *nchars* characters
                rather than waiting for a complete line of input.

-p *prompt*   Display *prompt*, without a trailing newline, be-
                fore attempting to read any input. The prompt
                is displayed only if input is coming from a ter-
                minal.

-r   If this option is given, backslash does not act
                as an escape character. The backslash is con-
                sidered to be part of the line. In particular,
                a backslash-newline pair may not be used as a
                line continuation.

-s   Silent mode. If input is coming from a termi-
                nal, characters are not echoed.

-t *timeout*   Cause read to time out and return failure if a
                complete line of input is not read within *time-
                out* seconds. This option has no effect if read is
                not reading input from the terminal or a pipe.

-u *fd*   Read input from file descriptor *fd*.

shopt

> shopt [-pqsu] [-o] [*optname* ...]
>
> Toggle the values of variables controlling optional shell behavior. With no options, or with the '-p' option, a list of all settable options is displayed, with an indication of whether or not each is set. The '-p' option causes output to be displayed in a form that may be reused as input. Other options have the following meanings:
>
> -s   Enable (set) each *optname*.
>
> -u   Disable (unset) each *optname*.
>
> -q   Suppresses normal output; the return status indicates whether the *optname* is set or unset. If multiple *optname* arguments are given with '-q', the return status is zero if all *optnames* are enabled; non-zero otherwise.
>
> -o   Restricts the values of *optname* to be those defined for the '-o' option to the set builtin (see Section 4.3 [The Set Builtin], page 66).
>
> If either '-s' or '-u' is used with no *optname* arguments, the display is limited to those options which are set or unset, respectively.
>
> Unless otherwise noted, the shopt options are disabled (off) by default.
>
> The return status when listing options is zero if all *optnames* are enabled, non-zero otherwise. When setting or unsetting options, the return status is zero unless an *optname* is not a valid shell option.
>
> The list of shopt options is:
>
> cdable_vars
>
> > If this is set, an argument to the cd builtin command that is not a directory is assumed to be the name of a variable whose value is the directory to change to.
>
> cdspell   If set, minor errors in the spelling of a directory component in a cd command will be corrected. The errors checked for are transposed characters, a missing character, and a character too many. If a correction is found, the corrected path is printed, and the command proceeds. This option is only used by interactive shells.

checkhash   If this is set, Bash checks that a command
             found in the hash table exists before trying to
             execute it. If a hashed command no longer ex-
             ists, a normal path search is performed.

checkwinsize
             If set, Bash checks the window size after each
             command and, if necessary, updates the values
             of LINES and COLUMNS.

cmdhist   If set, Bash attempts to save all lines of a
             multiple-line command in the same history en-
             try. This allows easy re-editing of multi-line
             commands.

dotglob   If set, Bash includes filenames beginning with
             a '.' in the results of filename expansion.

execfail   If this is set, a non-interactive shell will not
             exit if it cannot execute the file specified as an
             argument to the exec builtin command. An
             interactive shell does not exit if exec fails.

expand_aliases
             If set, aliases are expanded as described below
             under Aliases, Section 6.6 [Aliases], page 95.
             This option is enabled by default for interactive
             shells.

extdebug   If set, behavior intended for use by debuggers
             is enabled:

             1. The '-F' option to the declare builtin
                (see Section 4.2 [Bash Builtins], page 51)
                displays the source file name and line
                number corresponding to each function
                name supplied as an argument.

             2. If the command run by the DEBUG trap re-
                turns a non-zero value, the next command
                is skipped and not executed.

             3. If the command run by the DEBUG trap
                returns a value of 2, and the shell is exe-
                cuting in a subroutine (a shell function or
                a shell script executed by the . or source
                builtins), a call to return is simulated.

             4. BASH_ARGC and BASH_ARGV are updated as
                described in their descriptions (see Sec-
                tion 5.2 [Bash Variables], page 74).

5. Function tracing is enabled: command substitution, shell functions, and subshells invoked with (*command*) inherit the DEBUG and RETURN traps.

6. Error tracing is enabled: command substitution, shell functions, and subshells invoked with (*command*) inherit the ERROR trap.

extglob
> If set, the extended pattern matching features described above (see Section 3.5.8.1 [Pattern Matching], page 31) are enabled.

extquote
> If set, $'*string*' and $"*string*" quoting is performed within ${*parameter*} expansions enclosed in double quotes. This option is enabled by default.

failglob
> If set, patterns which fail to match filenames during pathname expansion result in an expansion error.

force_fignore
> If set, the suffixes specified by the FIGNORE shell variable cause words to be ignored when performing word completion even if the ignored words are the only possible completions. See Section 5.2 [Bash Variables], page 74, for a description of FIGNORE. This option is enabled by default.

gnu_errfmt
> If set, shell error messages are written in the standard GNU error message format.

histappend
> If set, the history list is appended to the file named by the value of the HISTFILE variable when the shell exits, rather than overwriting the file.

histreedit
> If set, and Readline is being used, a user is given the opportunity to re-edit a failed history substitution.

`histverify`

>If set, and Readline is being used, the re-
sults of history substitution are not immediately passed to the shell parser. Instead, the
resulting line is loaded into the Readline editing buffer, allowing further modification.

`hostcomplete`

>If set, and Readline is being used, Bash will at-
tempt to perform hostname completion when
a word containing a '@' is being completed
(see Section 8.4.6 [Commands For Completion],
page 133). This option is enabled by default.

`huponexit`   If set, Bash will send SIGHUP to all jobs when
an interactive login shell exits (see Section 3.7.6
[Signals], page 40).

`interactive_comments`

>Allow a word beginning with '#' to cause that
word and all remaining characters on that line
to be ignored in an interactive shell. This option is enabled by default.

`lithist`   If enabled, and the cmdhist option is enabled, multi-line commands are saved to the
history with embedded newlines rather than
using semicolon separators where possible.

`login_shell`

>The shell sets this option if it is started as
a login shell (see Section 6.1 [Invoking Bash],
page 85). The value may not be changed.

`mailwarn`   If set, and a file that Bash is checking for
mail has been accessed since the last time it
was checked, the message "The mail in *mail-
file* has been read" is displayed.

`no_empty_cmd_completion`

>If set, and Readline is being used, Bash will not
attempt to search the PATH for possible completions when completion is attempted on an
empty line.

`nocaseglob`

>If set, Bash matches filenames in a case-
insensitive fashion when performing filename
expansion.

nocasematch
> If set, Bash matches patterns in a case-insensitive fashion when performing matching while executing case or [[conditional commands.

nullglob
> If set, Bash allows filename patterns which match no files to expand to a null string, rather than themselves.

progcomp
> If set, the programmable completion facilities (see Section 8.6 [Programmable Completion], page 138) are enabled. This option is enabled by default.

promptvars
> If set, prompt strings undergo parameter expansion, command substitution, arithmetic expansion, and quote removal after being expanded as described below (see Section 6.9 [Printing a Prompt], page 99). This option is enabled by default.

restricted_shell
> The shell sets this option if it is started in restricted mode (see Section 6.10 [The Restricted Shell], page 101). The value may not be changed. This is not reset when the startup files are executed, allowing the startup files to discover whether or not a shell is restricted.

shift_verbose
> If this is set, the shift builtin prints an error message when the shift count exceeds the number of positional parameters.

sourcepath
> If set, the source builtin uses the value of PATH to find the directory containing the file supplied as an argument. This option is enabled by default.

xpg_echo
> If set, the echo builtin expands backslash-escape sequences by default.

The return status when listing options is zero if all *optnames* are enabled, non-zero otherwise. When setting or unsetting options, the return status is zero unless an *optname* is not a valid shell option.

source

> source *filename*

A synonym for . (see Section 4.1 [Bourne Shell Builtins], page 43).

type

> type [-afptP] [*name* ...]

For each *name*, indicate how it would be interpreted if used as a command name.

If the '-t' option is used, type prints a single word which is one of 'alias', 'function', 'builtin', 'file' or 'keyword', if *name* is an alias, shell function, shell builtin, disk file, or shell reserved word, respectively. If the *name* is not found, then nothing is printed, and type returns a failure status.

If the '-p' option is used, type either returns the name of the disk file that would be executed, or nothing if '-t' would not return 'file'.

The '-P' option forces a path search for each *name*, even if '-t' would not return 'file'.

If a command is hashed, '-p' and '-P' print the hashed value, not necessarily the file that appears first in $PATH.

If the '-a' option is used, type returns all of the places that contain an executable named *file*. This includes aliases and functions, if and only if the '-p' option is not also used.

If the '-f' option is used, type does not attempt to find shell functions, as with the command builtin.

The return status is zero if any of the *names* are found, non-zero if none are found.

typeset

> typeset [-afFrxi] [-p] [*name*[=*value*] ...]

The typeset command is supplied for compatibility with the Korn shell; however, it has been deprecated in favor of the declare builtin command.

ulimit

> ulimit [-acdefilmnpqrstuvxSH] [*limit*]

ulimit provides control over the resources available to processes started by the shell, on systems that allow such control. If an option is given, it is interpreted as follows:

-S	Change and report the soft limit associated with a resource.
-H	Change and report the hard limit associated with a resource.
-a	All current limits are reported.
-c	The maximum size of core files created.
-d	The maximum size of a process's data segment.
-e	The maximum scheduling priority ("nice").
-f	The maximum size of files written by the shell and its children.
-i	The maximum number of pending signals.
-l	The maximum size that may be locked into memory.
-m	The maximum resident set size.
-n	The maximum number of open file descriptors.
-p	The pipe buffer size.
-q	The maximum number of bytes in POSIX message queues.
-r	The maximum real-time scheduling priority.
-s	The maximum stack size.
-t	The maximum amount of cpu time in seconds.
-u	The maximum number of processes available to a single user.
-v	The maximum amount of virtual memory available to the process.
-x	The maximum number of file locks.

If *limit* is given, it is the new value of the specified resource; the special *limit* values hard, soft, and unlimited stand for the current hard limit, the current soft limit, and no limit, respectively. Otherwise, the current value of the soft limit for the specified resource is printed, unless the '-H' option is supplied. When setting new limits, if neither '-H' nor '-S' is supplied, both the hard and soft limits are set. If no option is given, then '-f' is assumed. Values are in 1024-byte

increments, except for '-t', which is in seconds, '-p', which
is in units of 512-byte blocks, and '-n' and '-u', which are
unscaled values.

The return status is zero unless an invalid option or argument is supplied, or an error occurs while setting a new limit.

unalias

unalias [-a] [*name* ...]

Remove each *name* from the list of aliases. If '-a' is supplied,
all aliases are removed. Aliases are described in Section 6.6
[Aliases], page 95.

4.3 The Set Builtin

This builtin is so complicated that it deserves its own section.

set

set [--abefhkmnptuvxBCHP] [-o *option*]
    [*argument* ...]

If no options or arguments are supplied, set displays the
names and values of all shell variables and functions, sorted
according to the current locale, in a format that may be
reused as input for setting or resetting the currently-set variables. Read-only variables cannot be reset. In POSIX mode,
only shell variables are listed.

When options are supplied, they set or unset shell attributes.
Options, if specified, have the following meanings:

-a   Mark variables and function which are modi-
            fied or created for export to the environment
            of subsequent commands.

-b   Cause the status of terminated background
            jobs to be reported immediately, rather than
            before printing the next primary prompt.

-e   Exit immediately if a simple command (see
            Section 3.2.1 [Simple Commands], page 10) ex-
            its with a non-zero status, unless the command
            that fails is part of the command list immedi-
            ately following a while or until keyword, part
            of the test in an if statement, part of a && or
            | | list, or if the command's return status is be-
            ing inverted using !. A trap on ERR, if set, is
            executed before the shell exits.

-f   Disable file name generation (globbing).

-h   Locate and remember (hash) commands as they are looked up for execution. This option is enabled by default.

-k   All arguments in the form of assignment statements are placed in the environment for a command, not just those that precede the command name.

-m   Job control is enabled (see Chapter 7 [Job Control], page 107).

-n   Read commands but do not execute them; this may be used to check a script for syntax errors. This option is ignored by interactive shells.

-o *option-name*

              Set the option corresponding to *option-name*:

              allexport   Same as -a.

              braceexpand
                          Same as -B.

              emacs   Use an emacs-style line editing interface (see Chapter 8 [Command Line Editing], page 113).

              errexit   Same as -e.

              errtrace   Same as -E.

              functrace   Same as -T.

              hashall   Same as -h.

              histexpand
                          Same as -H.

              history   Enable command history, as described in Section 9.1 [Bash History Facilities], page 145. This option is on by default in interactive shells.

              ignoreeof   An interactive shell will not exit upon reading EOF.

              keyword   Same as -k.

              monitor   Same as -m.

noclobber   Same as -C.

noexec   Same as -n.

noglob   Same as -f.

nolog   Currently ignored.

notify   Same as -b.

nounset   Same as -u.

onecmd   Same as -t.

physical   Same as -P.

pipefail   If set, the return value of a
             pipeline is the value of the last
             (rightmost) command to exit
             with a non-zero status, or zero
             if all commands in the pipeline
             exit successfully. This option is
             disabled by default.

posix   Change the behavior of Bash
             where the default operation
             differs from the POSIX standard
             to match the standard (see
             Section 6.11 [Bash POSIX
             Mode], page 102). This is
             intended to make Bash behave as
             a strict superset of that standard.

privileged
             Same as -p.

verbose   Same as -v.

vi   Use a vi-style line editing inter-
             face.

xtrace   Same as -x.

-p   Turn on privileged mode. In this mode, the
             $BASH_ENV and $ENV files are not processed,
             shell functions are not inherited from the en-
             vironment, and the SHELLOPTS variable, if it
             appears in the environment, is ignored. If the
             shell is started with the effective user (group)
             id not equal to the real user (group) id, and
             the -p option is not supplied, these actions are

taken and the effective user id is set to the real user id. If the -p option is supplied at startup, the effective user id is not reset. Turning this option off causes the effective user and group ids to be set to the real user and group ids.

-t   Exit after reading and executing one command.

-u   Treat unset variables as an error when performing parameter expansion. An error message will be written to the standard error, and a non-interactive shell will exit.

-v   Print shell input lines as they are read.

-x   Print a trace of simple commands, for commands, case commands, select commands, and arithmetic for commands and their arguments or associated word lists after they are expanded and before they are executed. The value of the PS4 variable is expanded and the resultant value is printed before the command and its expanded arguments.

-B   The shell will perform brace expansion (see Section 3.5.1 [Brace Expansion], page 23). This option is on by default.

-C   Prevent output redirection using '>', '>&', and '<>' from overwriting existing files.

-E   If set, any trap on ERR is inherited by shell functions, command substitutions, and commands executed in a subshell environment. The ERR trap is normally not inherited in such cases.

-H   Enable '!' style history substitution (see Section 9.3 [History Interaction], page 147). This option is on by default for interactive shells.

-P   If set, do not follow symbolic links when performing commands such as cd which change the current directory. The physical directory is used instead. By default, Bash follows the logical chain of directories when performing commands which change the current directory.

            For example, if '/usr/sys' is a symbolic link to '/usr/local/sys' then:

```
$ cd /usr/sys; echo $PWD
/usr/sys
$ cd ..; pwd
/usr
```

If set -P is on, then:

```
$ cd /usr/sys; echo $PWD
/usr/local/sys
$ cd ..; pwd
/usr/local
```

-T   If set, any trap on DEBUG and RETURN are inher-
            ited by shell functions, command substitutions,
            and commands executed in a subshell environ-
            ment. The DEBUG and RETURN traps are nor-
            mally not inherited in such cases.

--   If no arguments follow this option, then the po-
            sitional parameters are unset. Otherwise, the
            positional parameters are set to the *arguments*,
            even if some of them begin with a '-'.

-           Signal the end of options, cause all remaining
            arguments to be assigned to the positional pa-
            rameters. The '-x' and '-v' options are turned
            off. If there are no arguments, the positional
            parameters remain unchanged.

Using '+' rather than '-' causes these options to be turned
off. The options can also be used upon invocation of the
shell. The current set of options may be found in $-.

The remaining N *arguments* are positional parameters and
are assigned, in order, to $1, $2, ... $N. The special param-
eter # is set to N.

The return status is always zero unless an invalid option is
supplied.

4.4 Special Builtins

For historical reasons, the POSIX standard has classified several builtin
commands as *special*. When Bash is executing in POSIX mode, the special
builtins differ from other builtin commands in three respects:

1. Special builtins are found before shell functions during command
   lookup.

2. If a special builtin returns an error status, a non-interactive shell exits.

3. Assignment statements preceding the command stay in effect in the shell environment after the command completes.

When Bash is not executing in POSIX mode, these builtins behave no differently than the rest of the Bash builtin commands. The Bash POSIX mode is described in Section 6.11 [Bash POSIX Mode], page 102.

These are the POSIX special builtins:

```
break       :                       continue  eval      exec
exit        export    readonly      return    set       shift
trap        unset
```

5 Shell Variables

This chapter describes the shell variables that Bash uses. Bash automatically assigns default values to a number of variables.

5.1 Bourne Shell Variables

Bash uses certain shell variables in the same way as the Bourne shell. In some cases, Bash assigns a default value to the variable.

CDPATH   A colon-separated list of directories used as a search path for the cd builtin command.

HOME   The current user's home directory; the default for the cd builtin command. The value of this variable is also used by tilde expansion (see Section 3.5.2 [Tilde Expansion], page 24).

IFS   A list of characters that separate fields; used when the shell splits words as part of expansion.

MAIL   If this parameter is set to a filename and the MAILPATH variable is not set, Bash informs the user of the arrival of mail in the specified file.

MAILPATH   A colon-separated list of filenames which the shell periodically checks for new mail. Each list entry can specify the message that is printed when new mail arrives in the mail file by separating the file name from the message with a '?'. When used in the text of the message, $_ expands to the name of the current mail file.

OPTARG   The value of the last option argument processed by the getopts builtin.

OPTIND   The index of the last option argument processed by the getopts builtin.

PATH   A colon-separated list of directories in which the shell looks for commands. A zero-length (null) directory name in the value of PATH indicates the current directory. A null directory name may appear as two adjacent colons, or as an initial or trailing colon.

PS1   The primary prompt string. The default value is '\s-\v\$
             '. See Section 6.9 [Printing a Prompt], page 99, for the
             complete list of escape sequences that are expanded before
             PS1 is displayed.

PS2   The secondary prompt string. The default value is '> '.

5.2 Bash Variables

These variables are set or used by Bash, but other shells do not normally treat them specially.

A few variables used by Bash are described in different chapters: variables for controlling the job control facilities (see Section 7.3 [Job Control
Variables], page 110).

BASH   The full pathname used to execute the current instance of
             Bash.

BASH_ARGC   An array variable whose values are the number of parame-
             ters in each frame of the current bash execution call stack.
             The number of parameters to the current subroutine (shell
             function or script executed with . or source) is at the top
             of the stack. When a subroutine is executed, the number
             of parameters passed is pushed onto BASH_ARGC. The shell
             sets BASH_ARGC only when in extended debugging mode (see
             Section 4.2 [Bash Builtins], page 51 for a description of the
             extdebug option to the shopt builtin).

BASH_ARGV   An array variable containing all of the parameters in the
             current bash execution call stack. The final parameter of
             the last subroutine call is at the top of the stack; the first
             parameter of the initial call is at the bottom. When a sub-
             routine is executed, the parameters supplied are pushed onto
             BASH_ARGV. The shell sets BASH_ARGV only when in extended
             debugging mode (see Section 4.2 [Bash Builtins], page 51 for
             a description of the extdebug option to the shopt builtin).

BASH_COMMAND
             The command currently being executed or about to be exe-
             cuted, unless the shell is executing a command as the result
             of a trap, in which case it is the command executing at the
             time of the trap.

BASH_ENV   If this variable is set when Bash is invoked to execute a
             shell script, its value is expanded and used as the name of

a startup file to read before executing the script. See Section 6.2 [Bash Startup Files], page 87.

BASH_EXECUTION_STRING
>   The command argument to the '-c' invocation option.

BASH_LINENO
>   An array variable whose members are the line numbers in source files corresponding to each member of *FUNCNAME*. ${BASH_LINENO[$i]} is the line number in the source file where ${FUNCNAME[$i]} was called. The corresponding source file name is ${BASH_SOURCE[$i]}. Use LINENO to obtain the current line number.

BASH_REMATCH
>   An array variable whose members are assigned by the '=~' binary operator to the [[conditional command (see Section 3.2.4.2 [Conditional Constructs], page 14). The element with index 0 is the portion of the string matching the entire regular expression. The element with index *n* is the portion of the string matching the *n*th parenthesized subexpression. This variable is read-only.

BASH_SOURCE
>   An array variable whose members are the source filenames corresponding to the elements in the FUNCNAME array variable.

BASH_SUBSHELL
>   Incremented by one each time a subshell or subshell environment is spawned. The initial value is 0.

BASH_VERSINFO
>   A readonly array variable (see Section 6.7 [Arrays], page 96) whose members hold version information for this instance of Bash. The values assigned to the array members are as follows:

>   BASH_VERSINFO[0]
>>   The major version number (the *release*).

>   BASH_VERSINFO[1]
>>   The minor version number (the *version*).

>   BASH_VERSINFO[2]
>>   The patch level.

BASH_VERSINFO[3]
>   The build version.

BASH_VERSINFO[4]
>   The release status (e.g., *beta1*).

BASH_VERSINFO[5]
>   The value of MACHTYPE.

BASH_VERSION
>   The version number of the current instance of Bash.

COLUMNS   Used by the select builtin command to determine the ter-
>   minal width when printing selection lists. Automatically set
>   upon receipt of a SIGWINCH.

COMP_CWORD
>   An index into ${COMP_WORDS} of the word containing the
>   current cursor position. This variable is available only
>   in shell functions invoked by the programmable comple-
>   tion facilities (see Section 8.6 [Programmable Completion],
>   page 138).

COMP_LINE   The current command line. This variable is available only
>   in shell functions and external commands invoked by the
>   programmable completion facilities (see Section 8.6 [Pro-
>   grammable Completion], page 138).

COMP_POINT
>   The index of the current cursor position relative to the be-
>   ginning of the current command. If the current cursor posi-
>   tion is at the end of the current command, the value of this
>   variable is equal to ${#COMP_LINE}. This variable is avail-
>   able only in shell functions and external commands invoked
>   by the programmable completion facilities (see Section 8.6
>   [Programmable Completion], page 138).

COMP_WORDBREAKS
>   The set of characters that the Readline library treats as
>   word separators when performing word completion. If COMP_
>   WORDBREAKS is unset, it loses its special properties, even if it
>   is subsequently reset.

COMP_WORDS
>   An array variable consisting of the individual words in
>   the current command line. The words are split on shell

metacharacters as the shell parser would separate them. This variable is available only in shell functions invoked by the programmable completion facilities (see Section 8.6 [Programmable Completion], page 138).

COMPREPLY   An array variable from which Bash reads the possible completions generated by a shell function invoked by the programmable completion facility (see Section 8.6 [Programmable Completion], page 138).

DIRSTACK   An array variable containing the current contents of the directory stack. Directories appear in the stack in the order they are displayed by the `dirs` builtin. Assigning to members of this array variable may be used to modify directories already in the stack, but the `pushd` and `popd` builtins must be used to add and remove directories. Assignment to this variable will not change the current directory. If DIRSTACK is unset, it loses its special properties, even if it is subsequently reset.

EMACS   If Bash finds this variable in the environment when the shell starts with value 't', it assumes that the shell is running in an emacs shell buffer and disables line editing.

EUID   The numeric effective user id of the current user. This variable is readonly.

FCEDIT   The editor used as a default by the '-e' option to the `fc` builtin command.

FIGNORE   A colon-separated list of suffixes to ignore when performing filename completion. A file name whose suffix matches one of the entries in FIGNORE is excluded from the list of matched file names. A sample value is '.o:~'

FUNCNAME   An array variable containing the names of all shell functions currently in the execution call stack. The element with index 0 is the name of any currently-executing shell function. The bottom-most element is "main". This variable exists only when a shell function is executing. Assignments to FUNCNAME have no effect and return an error status. If FUNCNAME is unset, it loses its special properties, even if it is subsequently reset.

GLOBIGNORE
A colon-separated list of patterns defining the set of filenames to be ignored by filename expansion. If a filename

matched by a filename expansion pattern also matches one of the patterns in GLOBIGNORE, it is removed from the list of matches.

GROUPS   An array variable containing the list of groups of which the current user is a member. Assignments to GROUPS have no effect and return an error status. If GROUPS is unset, it loses its special properties, even if it is subsequently reset.

histchars   Up to three characters which control history expansion, quick substitution, and tokenization (see Section 9.3 [History Interaction], page 147). The first character is the *history expansion* character, that is, the character which signifies the start of a history expansion, normally '!'. The second character is the character which signifies 'quick substitution' when seen as the first character on a line, normally '^'. The optional third character is the character which indicates that the remainder of the line is a comment when found as the first character of a word, usually '#'. The history comment character causes history substitution to be skipped for the remaining words on the line. It does not necessarily cause the shell parser to treat the rest of the line as a comment.

HISTCMD   The history number, or index in the history list, of the current command. If HISTCMD is unset, it loses its special properties, even if it is subsequently reset.

HISTCONTROL
            A colon-separated list of values controlling how commands are saved on the history list. If the list of values includes 'ignorespace', lines which begin with a space character are not saved in the history list. A value of 'ignoredups' causes lines which match the previous history entry to not be saved. A value of 'ignoreboth' is shorthand for 'ignorespace' and 'ignoredups'. A value of 'erasedups' causes all previous lines matching the current line to be removed from the history list before that line is saved. Any value not in the above list is ignored. If HISTCONTROL is unset, or does not include a valid value, all lines read by the shell parser are saved on the history list, subject to the value of HISTIGNORE. The second and subsequent lines of a multi-line compound command are not tested, and are added to the history regardless of the value of HISTCONTROL.

HISTFILE   The name of the file to which the command history is saved. The default value is '~/.bash_history'.

HISTFILESIZE
>   The maximum number of lines contained in the history file.
>   When this variable is assigned a value, the history file is
>   truncated, if necessary, by removing the oldest entries, to
>   contain no more than that number of lines. The history
>   file is also truncated to this size after writing it when an
>   interactive shell exits. The default value is 500.

HISTIGNORE
>   A colon-separated list of patterns used to decide which com-
>   mand lines should be saved on the history list. Each pattern
>   is anchored at the beginning of the line and must match
>   the complete line (no implicit '*' is appended). Each pat-
>   tern is tested against the line after the checks specified by
>   HISTCONTROL are applied. In addition to the normal shell
>   pattern matching characters, '&' matches the previous his-
>   tory line. '&' may be escaped using a backslash; the back-
>   slash is removed before attempting a match. The second and
>   subsequent lines of a multi-line compound command are not
>   tested, and are added to the history regardless of the value
>   of HISTIGNORE.
>
>   HISTIGNORE subsumes the function of HISTCONTROL. A pat-
>   tern of '&' is identical to ignoredups, and a pattern of '[ ]*'
>   is identical to ignorespace. Combining these two patterns,
>   separating them with a colon, provides the functionality of
>   ignoreboth.

HISTSIZE   The maximum number of commands to remember on the
>   history list. The default value is 500.

HISTTIMEFORMAT
>   If this variable is set and not null, its value is used as a
>   format string for *strftime* to print the time stamp associated
>   with each history entry displayed by the history builtin. If
>   this variable is set, time stamps are written to the history
>   file so they may be preserved across shell sessions.

HOSTFILE   Contains the name of a file in the same format as
>   '/etc/hosts' that should be read when the shell needs
>   to complete a hostname. The list of possible hostname
>   completions may be changed while the shell is running;
>   the next time hostname completion is attempted after the
>   value is changed, Bash adds the contents of the new file
>   to the existing list. If HOSTFILE is set, but has no value,

Bash attempts to read '/etc/hosts' to obtain the list of possible hostname completions. When HOSTFILE is unset, the hostname list is cleared.

HOSTNAME   The name of the current host.

HOSTTYPE   A string describing the machine Bash is running on.

IGNOREEOF   Controls the action of the shell on receipt of an EOF character as the sole input. If set, the value denotes the number of consecutive EOF characters that can be read as the first character on an input line before the shell will exit. If the variable exists but does not have a numeric value (or has no value) then the default is 10. If the variable does not exist, then EOF signifies the end of input to the shell. This is only in effect for interactive shells.

INPUTRC   The name of the Readline initialization file, overriding the default of '~/.inputrc'.

LANG   Used to determine the locale category for any category not specifically selected with a variable starting with LC_.

LC_ALL   This variable overrides the value of LANG and any other LC_ variable specifying a locale category.

LC_COLLATE
            This variable determines the collation order used when sorting the results of filename expansion, and determines the behavior of range expressions, equivalence classes, and collating sequences within filename expansion and pattern matching (see Section 3.5.8 [Filename Expansion], page 30).

LC_CTYPE   This variable determines the interpretation of characters and the behavior of character classes within filename expansion and pattern matching (see Section 3.5.8 [Filename Expansion], page 30).

LC_MESSAGES
            This variable determines the locale used to translate double-quoted strings preceded by a '$' (see Section 3.1.2.5 [Locale Translation], page 10).

LC_NUMERIC
            This variable determines the locale category used for number formatting.

LINENO   The line number in the script or shell function currently executing.

LINES   Used by the select builtin command to determine the column length for printing selection lists. Automatically set upon receipt of a SIGWINCH.

MACHTYPE   A string that fully describes the system type on which Bash is executing, in the standard GNU *cpu-company-system* format.

MAILCHECK   How often (in seconds) that the shell should check for mail in the files specified in the MAILPATH or MAIL variables. The default is 60 seconds. When it is time to check for mail, the shell does so before displaying the primary prompt. If this variable is unset, or set to a value that is not a number greater than or equal to zero, the shell disables mail checking.

OLDPWD   The previous working directory as set by the cd builtin.

OPTERR   If set to the value 1, Bash displays error messages generated by the getopts builtin command.

OSTYPE   A string describing the operating system Bash is running on.

PIPESTATUS
            An array variable (see Section 6.7 [Arrays], page 96) containing a list of exit status values from the processes in the most-recently-executed foreground pipeline (which may contain only a single command).

POSIXLY_CORRECT
            If this variable is in the environment when bash starts, the shell enters POSIX mode (see Section 6.11 [Bash POSIX Mode], page 102) before reading the startup files, as if the '--posix' invocation option had been supplied. If it is set while the shell is running, bash enables POSIX mode, as if the command

                set -o posix

            had been executed.

PPID   The process ID of the shell's parent process. This variable is readonly.

PROMPT_COMMAND
            If set, the value is interpreted as a command to execute before the printing of each primary prompt ($PS1).

PS3   The value of this variable is used as the prompt for the
               select command. If this variable is not set, the select
               command prompts with '#? '

PS4   The value is the prompt printed before the command line is
               echoed when the '-x' option is set (see Section 4.3 [The Set
               Builtin], page 66). The first character of PS4 is replicated
               multiple times, as necessary, to indicate multiple levels of
               indirection. The default is '+ '.

PWD   The current working directory as set by the cd builtin.

RANDOM   Each time this parameter is referenced, a random integer
               between 0 and 32767 is generated. Assigning a value to this
               variable seeds the random number generator.

REPLY   The default variable for the read builtin.

SECONDS   This variable expands to the number of seconds since the
               shell was started. Assignment to this variable resets the
               count to the value assigned, and the expanded value be-
               comes the value assigned plus the number of seconds since
               the assignment.

SHELL   The full pathname to the shell is kept in this environment
               variable. If it is not set when the shell starts, Bash assigns
               to it the full pathname of the current user's login shell.

SHELLOPTS   A colon-separated list of enabled shell options. Each word
               in the list is a valid argument for the '-o' option to the set
               builtin command (see Section 4.3 [The Set Builtin], page 66).
               The options appearing in SHELLOPTS are those reported as
               'on' by 'set -o'. If this variable is in the environment when
               Bash starts up, each shell option in the list will be enabled
               before reading any startup files. This variable is readonly.

SHLVL   Incremented by one each time a new instance of Bash is
               started. This is intended to be a count of how deeply your
               Bash shells are nested.

TIMEFORMAT
               The value of this parameter is used as a format string speci-
               fying how the timing information for pipelines prefixed with
               the time reserved word should be displayed. The '%' charac-
               ter introduces an escape sequence that is expanded to a time
               value or other information. The escape sequences and their
               meanings are as follows; the braces denote optional portions.

%%   A literal '%'.

%[p][l]R   The elapsed time in seconds.

%[p][l]U   The number of CPU seconds spent in user mode.

%[p][l]S   The number of CPU seconds spent in system mode.

%P   The CPU percentage, computed as (%U + %S) / %R.

The optional p is a digit specifying the precision, the number of fractional digits after a decimal point. A value of 0 causes no decimal point or fraction to be output. At most three places after the decimal point may be specified; values of p greater than 3 are changed to 3. If p is not specified, the value 3 is used.

The optional l specifies a longer format, including minutes, of the form $MMmSS.FFs$. The value of p determines whether or not the fraction is included.

If this variable is not set, Bash acts as if it had the value

        $'\nreal\t%3lR\nuser\t%3lU\nsys\t%3lS'

If the value is null, no timing information is displayed. A trailing newline is added when the format string is displayed.

TMOUT   If set to a value greater than zero, TMOUT is treated as the default timeout for the read builtin (see Section 4.2 [Bash Builtins], page 51). The select command (see Section 3.2.4.2 [Conditional Constructs], page 14) terminates if input does not arrive after TMOUT seconds when input is coming from a terminal.

             In an interactive shell, the value is interpreted as the number of seconds to wait for input after issuing the primary prompt when the shell is interactive. Bash terminates after that number of seconds if input does not arrive.

TMPDIR   If set, Bash uses its value as the name of a directory in which Bash creates temporary files for the shell's use.

UID   The numeric real user id of the current user. This variable is readonly.

6 Bash Features

This section describes features unique to Bash.

6.1 Invoking Bash

```
bash [long-opt] [-ir] [-abefhkmnptuvxdBCDHP] [-o option]
    [-O shopt_option] [argument ...]
bash [long-opt] [-abefhkmnptuvxdBCDHP] [-o option]
    [-O shopt_option] -c string [argument ...]
bash [long-opt] -s [-abefhkmnptuvxdBCDHP] [-o option]
    [-O shopt_option] [argument ...]
```

In addition to the single-character shell command-line options (see Section 4.3 [The Set Builtin], page 66), there are several multi-character options that you can use. These options must appear on the command line before the single-character options to be recognized.

`--debugger`

> Arrange for the debugger profile to be executed before the shell starts. Turns on extended debugging mode (see Section 4.2 [Bash Builtins], page 51 for a description of the extdebug option to the shopt builtin) and shell function tracing (see Section 4.3 [The Set Builtin], page 66 for a description of the -o functrace option).

`--dump-po-strings`

> A list of all double-quoted strings preceded by '$' is printed on the standard output in the GNU gettext PO (portable object) file format. Equivalent to '-D' except for the output format.

`--dump-strings`

> Equivalent to '-D'.

`--help`   Display a usage message on standard output and exit successfully.

`--init-file` *filename*
`--rcfile` *filename*

> Execute commands from *filename* (instead of '~/.bashrc') in an interactive shell.

`--login`   Equivalent to '-l'.

`--noediting`
>   Do not use the GNU Readline library (see Chapter 8 [Command Line Editing], page 113) to read command lines when the shell is interactive.

`--noprofile`
>   Don't load the system-wide startup file '/etc/profile' or any of the personal initialization files '~/.bash_profile', '~/.bash_login', or '~/.profile' when Bash is invoked as a login shell.

`--norc` Don't read the '~/.bashrc' initialization file in an interactive shell. This is on by default if the shell is invoked as sh.

`--posix` Change the behavior of Bash where the default operation differs from the POSIX standard to match the standard. This is intended to make Bash behave as a strict superset of that standard. See Section 6.11 [Bash POSIX Mode], page 102, for a description of the Bash POSIX mode.

`--restricted`
>   Make the shell a restricted shell (see Section 6.10 [The Restricted Shell], page 101).

`--verbose` Equivalent to '-v'. Print shell input lines as they're read.

`--version` Show version information for this instance of Bash on the standard output and exit successfully.

There are several single-character options that may be supplied at invocation which are not available with the set builtin.

`-c string` Read and execute commands from *string* after processing the options, then exit. Any remaining arguments are assigned to the positional parameters, starting with $0.

`-i`   Force the shell to run interactively. Interactive shells are described in Section 6.3 [Interactive Shells], page 90.

`-l`   Make this shell act as if it had been directly invoked by login. When the shell is interactive, this is equivalent to starting a login shell with 'exec -l bash'. When the shell is not interactive, the login shell startup files will be executed. 'exec bash -l' or 'exec bash --login' will replace the current shell with a Bash login shell. See Section 6.2 [Bash Startup Files], page 87, for a description of the special behavior of a login shell.

`-r`   Make the shell a restricted shell (see Section 6.10 [The Restricted Shell], page 101).

-s   If this option is present, or if no arguments remain after op-
                tion processing, then commands are read from the standard
                input. This option allows the positional parameters to be
                set when invoking an interactive shell.

-D   A list of all double-quoted strings preceded by '$' is printed
                on the standard output. These are the strings that are sub-
                ject to language translation when the current locale is not C
                or POSIX (see Section 3.1.2.5 [Locale Translation], page 10).
                This implies the '-n' option; no commands will be executed.

[-+]O [shopt_option]
                shopt_option is one of the shell options accepted by the
                shopt builtin (see Chapter 4 [Shell Builtin Commands],
                page 43). If shopt_option is present, '-O' sets the value of
                that option; '+O' unsets it. If shopt_option is not supplied,
                the names and values of the shell options accepted by shopt
                are printed on the standard output. If the invocation op-
                tion is '+O', the output is displayed in a format that may be
                reused as input.

--   A -- signals the end of options and disables further option
                processing. Any arguments after the -- are treated as file-
                names and arguments.

A *login* shell is one whose first character of argument zero is '-', or
one invoked with the '--login' option.

An *interactive* shell is one started without non-option arguments,
unless '-s' is specified, without specifying the '-c' option, and whose
input and output are both connected to terminals (as determined by
isatty(3)), or one started with the '-i' option. See Section 6.3 [In-
teractive Shells], page 90, for more information.

If arguments remain after option processing, and neither the '-c' nor
the '-s' option has been supplied, the first argument is assumed to be the
name of a file containing shell commands (see Section 3.8 [Shell Scripts],
page 41). When Bash is invoked in this fashion, $0 is set to the name of
the file, and the positional parameters are set to the remaining arguments.
Bash reads and executes commands from this file, then exits. Bash's exit
status is the exit status of the last command executed in the script. If no
commands are executed, the exit status is 0.

6.2 Bash Startup Files

This section describes how Bash executes its startup files. If any of the
files exist but cannot be read, Bash reports an error. Tildes are expanded

in file names as described above under Tilde Expansion (see Section 3.5.2 [Tilde Expansion], page 24).

Interactive shells are described in Section 6.3 [Interactive Shells], page 90.

Invoked as an interactive login shell, or with '--login'

When Bash is invoked as an interactive login shell, or as a non-interactive shell with the '--login' option, it first reads and executes commands from the file '/etc/profile', if that file exists. After reading that file, it looks for '~/.bash_profile', '~/.bash_login', and '~/.profile', in that order, and reads and executes commands from the first one that exists and is readable. The '--noprofile' option may be used when the shell is started to inhibit this behavior.

When a login shell exits, Bash reads and executes commands from the file '~/.bash_logout', if it exists.

Invoked as an interactive non-login shell

When an interactive shell that is not a login shell is started, Bash reads and executes commands from '~/.bashrc', if that file exists. This may be inhibited by using the '--norc' option. The '--rcfile *file*' option will force Bash to read and execute commands from *file* instead of '~/.bashrc'.

So, typically, your '~/.bash_profile' contains the line

```
if [ -f ~/.bashrc ]; then . ~/.bashrc; fi
```

after (or before) any login-specific initializations.

Invoked non-interactively

When Bash is started non-interactively, to run a shell script, for example, it looks for the variable BASH_ENV in the environment, expands its value if it appears there, and uses the expanded value as the name of a file to read and execute. Bash behaves as if the following command were executed:

```
if [ -n "$BASH_ENV" ]; then . "$BASH_ENV"; fi
```

but the value of the PATH variable is not used to search for the file name.

As noted above, if a non-interactive shell is invoked with the '--login' option, Bash attempts to read and execute commands from the login shell startup files.

Invoked with name sh

If Bash is invoked with the name sh, it tries to mimic the startup behavior of historical versions of sh as closely as possible, while conforming to the POSIX standard as well.

When invoked as an interactive login shell, or as a non-interactive shell with the '--login' option, it first attempts to read and execute commands from '/etc/profile' and '~/.profile', in that order. The '--noprofile' option may be used to inhibit this behavior. When invoked as an interactive shell with the name sh, Bash looks for the variable ENV, expands its value if it is defined, and uses the expanded value as the name of a file to read and execute. Since a shell invoked as sh does not attempt to read and execute commands from any other startup files, the '--rcfile' option has no effect. A non-interactive shell invoked with the name sh does not attempt to read any other startup files.

When invoked as sh, Bash enters POSIX mode after the startup files are read.

Invoked in POSIX mode

When Bash is started in POSIX mode, as with the '--posix' command line option, it follows the POSIX standard for startup files. In this mode, interactive shells expand the ENV variable and commands are read and executed from the file whose name is the expanded value. No other startup files are read.

Invoked by remote shell daemon

Bash attempts to determine when it is being run by the remote shell daemon, usually rshd. If Bash determines it is being run by rshd, it reads and executes commands from '~/.bashrc', if that file exists and is readable. It will not do this if invoked as sh. The '--norc' option may be used to inhibit this behavior, and the '--rcfile' option may be used to force another file to be read, but rshd does not generally invoke the shell with those options or allow them to be specified.

Invoked with unequal effective and real UID/GIDS

If Bash is started with the effective user (group) id not equal to the real user (group) id, and the -p option is not supplied, no startup files are read, shell functions are not inherited from the environment, the SHELLOPTS variable, if it appears in the environment, is ignored, and the effective user id is set to the real user id. If the -p option is supplied at invocation, the startup behavior is the same, but the effective user id is not reset.

6.3 Interactive Shells

6.3.1 What is an Interactive Shell?

An interactive shell is one started without non-option arguments, unless '-s' is specified, without specifying the '-c' option, and whose input and error output are both connected to terminals (as determined by isatty(3)), or one started with the '-i' option.

An interactive shell generally reads from and writes to a user's terminal.

The '-s' invocation option may be used to set the positional parameters when an interactive shell is started.

6.3.2 Is this Shell Interactive?

To determine within a startup script whether or not Bash is running interactively, test the value of the '-' special parameter. It contains i when the shell is interactive. For example:

```
case "$-" in
*i*) echo This shell is interactive ;;
*) echo This shell is not interactive ;;
esac
```

Alternatively, startup scripts may examine the variable PS1; it is unset in non-interactive shells, and set in interactive shells. Thus:

```
if [ -z "$PS1" ]; then
        echo This shell is not interactive
else
        echo This shell is interactive
fi
```

6.3.3 Interactive Shell Behavior

When the shell is running interactively, it changes its behavior in several ways.

1. Startup files are read and executed as described in Section 6.2 [Bash Startup Files], page 87.

2. Job Control (see Chapter 7 [Job Control], page 107) is enabled by default. When job control is in effect, Bash ignores the keyboard-generated job control signals SIGTTIN, SIGTTOU, and SIGTSTP.

3. Bash expands and displays PS1 before reading the first line of a command, and expands and displays PS2 before reading the second and subsequent lines of a multi-line command.

4. Bash executes the value of the PROMPT_COMMAND variable as a command before printing the primary prompt, $PS1 (see Section 5.2 [Bash Variables], page 74).

5. Readline (see Chapter 8 [Command Line Editing], page 113) is used to read commands from the user's terminal.

6. Bash inspects the value of the ignoreeof option to set -o instead of exiting immediately when it receives an EOF on its standard input when reading a command (see Section 4.3 [The Set Builtin], page 66).

7. Command history (see Section 9.1 [Bash History Facilities], page 145) and history expansion (see Section 9.3 [History Interaction], page 147) are enabled by default. Bash will save the command history to the file named by $HISTFILE when an interactive shell exits.

8. Alias expansion (see Section 6.6 [Aliases], page 95) is performed by default.

9. In the absence of any traps, Bash ignores SIGTERM (see Section 3.7.6 [Signals], page 40).

10. In the absence of any traps, SIGINT is caught and handled ((see Section 3.7.6 [Signals], page 40). SIGINT will interrupt some shell builtins.

11. An interactive login shell sends a SIGHUP to all jobs on exit if the huponexit shell option has been enabled (see Section 3.7.6 [Signals], page 40).

12. The '-n' invocation option is ignored, and 'set -n' has no effect (see Section 4.3 [The Set Builtin], page 66).

13. Bash will check for mail periodically, depending on the values of the MAIL, MAILPATH, and MAILCHECK shell variables (see Section 5.2 [Bash Variables], page 74).

14. Expansion errors due to references to unbound shell variables after 'set -u' has been enabled will not cause the shell to exit (see Section 4.3 [The Set Builtin], page 66).

15. The shell will not exit on expansion errors caused by var being unset or null in ${var:?word} expansions (see Section 3.5.3 [Shell Parameter Expansion], page 25).

16. Redirection errors encountered by shell builtins will not cause the shell to exit.

17. When running in POSIX mode, a special builtin returning an error
    status will not cause the shell to exit (see Section 6.11 [Bash POSIX
    Mode], page 102).

18. A failed exec will not cause the shell to exit (see Section 4.1 [Bourne
    Shell Builtins], page 43).

19. Parser syntax errors will not cause the shell to exit.

20. Simple spelling correction for directory arguments to the cd builtin
    is enabled by default (see the description of the cdspell option to
    the shopt builtin in Section 4.2 [Bash Builtins], page 51).

21. The shell will check the value of the TMOUT variable and exit if a
    command is not read within the specified number of seconds after
    printing $PS1 (see Section 5.2 [Bash Variables], page 74).

6.4 Bash Conditional Expressions

M

Conditional expressions are used by the [[compound command and
the test and [builtin commands.

Expressions may be unary or binary. Unary expressions are often used
to examine the status of a file. There are string operators and numeric
comparison operators as well. If the *file* argument to one of the primaries
is of the form '/dev/fd/*N*', then file descriptor *N* is checked. If the *file*
argument to one of the primaries is one of '/dev/stdin', '/dev/stdout',
or '/dev/stderr', file descriptor 0, 1, or 2, respectively, is checked.

Unless otherwise specified, primaries that operate on files follow symbolic links and operate on the target of the link, rather than the link
itself.

-a *file*   True if *file* exists.

-b *file*   True if *file* exists and is a block special file.

-c *file*   True if *file* exists and is a character special file.

-d *file*   True if *file* exists and is a directory.

-e *file*   True if *file* exists.

-f *file*   True if *file* exists and is a regular file.

-g *file*   True if *file* exists and its set-group-id bit is set.

-h *file*   True if *file* exists and is a symbolic link.

-k *file*   True if *file* exists and its "sticky" bit is set.

-p *file*   True if *file* exists and is a named pipe (FIFO).

-r *file*　　　True if *file* exists and is readable.

-s *file*　　　True if *file* exists and has a size greater than zero.

-t *fd*　　　True if file descriptor *fd* is open and refers to a terminal.

-u *file*　　　True if *file* exists and its set-user-id bit is set.

-w *file*　　　True if *file* exists and is writable.

-x *file*　　　True if *file* exists and is executable.

-O *file*　　　True if *file* exists and is owned by the effective user id.

-G *file*　　　True if *file* exists and is owned by the effective group id.

-L *file*　　　True if *file* exists and is a symbolic link.

-S *file*　　　True if *file* exists and is a socket.

-N *file*　　　True if *file* exists and has been modified since it was last read.

file1 -nt *file2*
> True if *file1* is newer (according to modification date) than *file2*, or if *file1* exists and *file2* does not.

file1 -ot *file2*
> True if *file1* is older than *file2*, or if *file2* exists and *file1* does not.

file1 -ef *file2*
> True if *file1* and *file2* refer to the same device and inode numbers.

-o *optname*
> True if shell option *optname* is enabled. The list of options appears in the description of the '-o' option to the set builtin (see Section 4.3 [The Set Builtin], page 66).

-z *string*　　　True if the length of *string* is zero.

-n *string*
string　　　True if the length of *string* is non-zero.

string1 == *string2*
> True if the strings are equal. '=' may be used in place of '==' for strict POSIX compliance.

string1 != *string2*
> True if the strings are not equal.

string1 < *string2*
> True if *string1* sorts before *string2* lexicographically in the current locale.

string1 > *string2*
> True if *string1* sorts after *string2* lexicographically in the current locale.

arg1 OP *arg2*
> OP is one of '-eq', '-ne', '-lt', '-le', '-gt', or '-ge'. These arithmetic binary operators return true if *arg1* is equal to, not equal to, less than, less than or equal to, greater than, or greater than or equal to *arg2*, respectively. *Arg1* and *arg2* may be positive or negative integers.

6.5 Shell Arithmetic

The shell allows arithmetic expressions to be evaluated, as one of the shell expansions or by the let and the '-i' option to the declare builtins.

Evaluation is done in fixed-width integers with no check for overflow, though division by 0 is trapped and flagged as an error. The operators and their precedence, associativity, and values are the same as in the C language. The following list of operators is grouped into levels of equal-precedence operators. The levels are listed in order of decreasing precedence.

id++ *id*--
: variable post-increment and post-decrement

++*id* --*id*
: variable pre-increment and pre-decrement

- +
: unary minus and plus

! ~
: logical and bitwise negation

**
: exponentiation

* / %
: multiplication, division, remainder

+ -
: addition, subtraction

<< >>
: left and right bitwise shifts

<= >= < >
: comparison

== !=
: equality and inequality

&
: bitwise AND

^
: bitwise exclusive OR

|
: bitwise OR

&&   logical AND

|| logical OR

expr ? expr : expr
                conditional operator

= *= /= %= += -= <<= >>= &= ^= |=
                assignment

expr1 , expr2
                comma

Shell variables are allowed as operands; parameter expansion is performed before the expression is evaluated. Within an expression, shell variables may also be referenced by name without using the parameter expansion syntax. A shell variable that is null or unset evaluates to 0 when referenced by name without using the parameter expansion syntax. The value of a variable is evaluated as an arithmetic expression when it is referenced, or when a variable which has been given the *integer* attribute using 'declare -i' is assigned a value. A null value evaluates to 0. A shell variable need not have its integer attribute turned on to be used in an expression.

Constants with a leading 0 are interpreted as octal numbers. A leading '0x' or '0X' denotes hexadecimal. Otherwise, numbers take the form [*base#*]*n*, where *base* is a decimal number between 2 and 64 representing the arithmetic base, and *n* is a number in that base. If *base#* is omitted, then base 10 is used. The digits greater than 9 are represented by the lowercase letters, the uppercase letters, '@', and '_', in that order. If *base* is less than or equal to 36, lowercase and uppercase letters may be used interchangeably to represent numbers between 10 and 35.

Operators are evaluated in order of precedence. Sub-expressions in parentheses are evaluated first and may override the precedence rules above.

6.6 Aliases

Aliases allow a string to be substituted for a word when it is used as the first word of a simple command. The shell maintains a list of aliases that may be set and unset with the alias and unalias builtin commands.

The first word of each simple command, if unquoted, is checked to see if it has an alias. If so, that word is replaced by the text of the alias. The characters '/', '$', '`', '=' and any of the shell metacharacters or quoting characters listed above may not appear in an alias name. The replacement text may contain any valid shell input, including shell metacharacters.

The first word of the replacement text is tested for aliases, but a word that is identical to an alias being expanded is not expanded a second time. This means that one may alias ls to "ls -F", for instance, and Bash does not try to recursively expand the replacement text. If the last character of the alias value is a space or tab character, then the next command word following the alias is also checked for alias expansion.

Aliases are created and listed with the alias command, and removed with the unalias command.

There is no mechanism for using arguments in the replacement text, as in csh. If arguments are needed, a shell function should be used (see Section 3.3 [Shell Functions], page 18).

Aliases are not expanded when the shell is not interactive, unless the expand_aliases shell option is set using shopt (see Section 4.2 [Bash Builtins], page 51).

The rules concerning the definition and use of aliases are somewhat confusing. Bash always reads at least one complete line of input before executing any of the commands on that line. Aliases are expanded when a command is read, not when it is executed. Therefore, an alias definition appearing on the same line as another command does not take effect until the next line of input is read. The commands following the alias definition on that line are not affected by the new alias. This behavior is also an issue when functions are executed. Aliases are expanded when a function definition is read, not when the function is executed, because a function definition is itself a compound command. As a consequence, aliases defined in a function are not available until after that function is executed. To be safe, always put alias definitions on a separate line, and do not use alias in compound commands.

For almost every purpose, shell functions are preferred over aliases.

6.7 Arrays

Bash provides one-dimensional array variables. Any variable may be used as an array; the declare builtin will explicitly declare an array. There is no maximum limit on the size of an array, nor any requirement that members be indexed or assigned contiguously. Arrays are zero-based.

An array is created automatically if any variable is assigned to using the syntax

name[subscript]=value

The subscript is treated as an arithmetic expression that must evaluate to a number greater than or equal to zero. To explicitly declare an array, use

```
declare -a name
```

The syntax

```
declare -a name[subscript]
```

is also accepted; the *subscript* is ignored. Attributes may be specified for an array variable using the `declare` and `readonly` builtins. Each attribute applies to all members of an array.

Arrays are assigned to using compound assignments of the form

```
name=(value1 ... valuen)
```

where each *value* is of the form *[[subscript]=]string*. If the optional subscript is supplied, that index is assigned to; otherwise the index of the element assigned is the last index assigned to by the statement plus one. Indexing starts at zero. This syntax is also accepted by the `declare` builtin. Individual array elements may be assigned to using the *name[subscript]=value* syntax introduced above.

Any element of an array may be referenced using ${name[*subscript*]}. The braces are required to avoid conflicts with the shell's filename expansion operators. If the *subscript* is '@' or '*', the word expands to all members of the array *name*. These subscripts differ only when the word appears within double quotes. If the word is double-quoted, ${name[*]} expands to a single word with the value of each array member separated by the first character of the IFS variable, and ${name[@]} expands each element of *name* to a separate word. When there are no array members, ${name[@]} expands to nothing. If the double-quoted expansion occurs within a word, the expansion of the first parameter is joined with the beginning part of the original word, and the expansion of the last parameter is joined with the last part of the original word. This is analogous to the expansion of the special parameters '@' and '*'. ${#name[*subscript*]} expands to the length of ${name[*subscript*]}. If *subscript* is '@' or '*', the expansion is the number of elements in the array. Referencing an array variable without a subscript is equivalent to referencing element zero.

The unset builtin is used to destroy arrays. unset *name[subscript]* destroys the array element at index *subscript*. Care must be taken to avoid unwanted side effects caused by filename generation. unset *name*, where *name* is an array, removes the entire array. A subscript of '*' or '@' also removes the entire array.

The declare, local, and readonly builtins each accept a '-a' option to specify an array. The read builtin accepts a '-a' option to assign a list of words read from the standard input to an array, and can read values from the standard input into individual array elements. The set and declare builtins display array values in a way that allows them to be reused as input.

6.8 The Directory Stack

The directory stack is a list of recently-visited directories. The pushd builtin adds directories to the stack as it changes the current directory, and the popd builtin removes specified directories from the stack and changes the current directory to the directory removed. The dirs builtin displays the contents of the directory stack.

The contents of the directory stack are also visible as the value of the DIRSTACK shell variable.

6.8.1 Directory Stack Builtins

dirs

> dirs [+*N* | -*N*] [-clpv]
>
> Display the list of currently remembered directories. Directories are added to the list with the pushd command; the popd command removes directories from the list.
>
> +*N*   Displays the *N*th directory (counting from the left of the list printed by dirs when invoked without options), starting with zero.
>
> -*N*   Displays the *N*th directory (counting from the right of the list printed by dirs when invoked without options), starting with zero.
>
> -c   Clears the directory stack by deleting all of the elements.
>
> -l   Produces a longer listing; the default listing format uses a tilde to denote the home directory.
>
> -p   Causes dirs to print the directory stack with one entry per line.
>
> -v   Causes dirs to print the directory stack with one entry per line, prefixing each entry with its index in the stack.

popd

> popd [+*N* | -*N*] [-n]
>
> Remove the top entry from the directory stack, and cd to the new top directory. When no arguments are given, popd removes the top directory from the stack and performs a cd to the new top directory. The elements are numbered from

0 starting at the first directory listed with dirs; i.e., popd is equivalent to popd +0.

+*N*   Removes the *N*th directory (counting from the left of the list printed by dirs), starting with zero.

-*N*   Removes the *N*th directory (counting from the right of the list printed by dirs), starting with zero.

-n   Suppresses the normal change of directory when removing directories from the stack, so that only the stack is manipulated.

pushd

pushd [*dir* | +*N* | -*N*] [-n]

Save the current directory on the top of the directory stack and then cd to *dir*. With no arguments, pushd exchanges the top two directories.

+*N*   Brings the *N*th directory (counting from the left of the list printed by dirs, starting with zero) to the top of the list by rotating the stack.

-*N*   Brings the *N*th directory (counting from the right of the list printed by dirs, starting with zero) to the top of the list by rotating the stack.

-n   Suppresses the normal change of directory when adding directories to the stack, so that only the stack is manipulated.

dir   Makes the current working directory be the top of the stack, and then executes the equivalent of 'cd *dir*'. cds to *dir*.

6.9 Controlling the Prompt

The value of the variable PROMPT_COMMAND is examined just before Bash prints each primary prompt. If PROMPT_COMMAND is set and has a non-null value, then the value is executed just as if it had been typed on the command line.

In addition, the following table describes the special characters which can appear in the prompt variables:

\a   A bell character.

\d	The date, in "Weekday Month Date" format (e.g., "Tue May 26").
\D{*format*}	The *format* is passed to strftime(3) and the result is inserted into the prompt string; an empty *format* results in a locale-specific time representation. The braces are required.
\e	An escape character.
\h	The hostname, up to the first '.'.
\H	The hostname.
\j	The number of jobs currently managed by the shell.
\l	The basename of the shell's terminal device name.
\n	A newline.
\r	A carriage return.
\s	The name of the shell, the basename of $0 (the portion following the final slash).
\t	The time, in 24-hour HH:MM:SS format.
\T	The time, in 12-hour HH:MM:SS format.
\@	The time, in 12-hour am/pm format.
\A	The time, in 24-hour HH:MM format.
\u	The username of the current user.
\v	The version of Bash (e.g., 2.00)
\V	The release of Bash, version + patchlevel (e.g., 2.00.0)
\w	The current working directory, with $HOME abbreviated with a tilde.
\W	The basename of $PWD, with $HOME abbreviated with a tilde.
\!	The history number of this command.
\#	The command number of this command.
\$	If the effective uid is 0, #, otherwise $.
\nnn	The character whose ASCII code is the octal value *nnn*.
\\	A backslash.
\[	Begin a sequence of non-printing characters. This could be used to embed a terminal control sequence into the prompt.

\]   End a sequence of non-printing characters.

The command number and the history number are usually different: the history number of a command is its position in the history list, which may include commands restored from the history file (see Section 9.1 [Bash History Facilities], page 145), while the command number is the position in the sequence of commands executed during the current shell session.

After the string is decoded, it is expanded via parameter expansion, command substitution, arithmetic expansion, and quote removal, subject to the value of the promptvars shell option (see Section 4.2 [Bash Builtins], page 51).

6.10 The Restricted Shell

If Bash is started with the name rbash, or the '--restricted' or '-r' option is supplied at invocation, the shell becomes restricted. A restricted shell is used to set up an environment more controlled than the standard shell. A restricted shell behaves identically to bash with the exception that the following are disallowed or not performed:

- Changing directories with the cd builtin.
- Setting or unsetting the values of the SHELL, PATH, ENV, or BASH_ENV variables.
- Specifying command names containing slashes.
- Specifying a filename containing a slash as an argument to the . builtin command.
- Specifying a filename containing a slash as an argument to the '-p' option to the hash builtin command.
- Importing function definitions from the shell environment at startup.
- Parsing the value of SHELLOPTS from the shell environment at startup.
- Redirecting output using the '>', '>|', '<>', '>&', '&>', and '>>' redirection operators.
- Using the exec builtin to replace the shell with another command.
- Adding or deleting builtin commands with the '-f' and '-d' options to the enable builtin.
- Using the enable builtin command to enable disabled shell builtins.
- Specifying the '-p' option to the command builtin.
- Turning off restricted mode with 'set +r' or 'set +o restricted'.

These restrictions are enforced after any startup files are read.

When a command that is found to be a shell script is executed (see Section 3.8 [Shell Scripts], page 41), rbash turns off any restrictions in the shell spawned to execute the script.

6.11 Bash POSIX Mode

Starting Bash with the '--posix' command-line option or executing 'set -o posix' while Bash is running will cause Bash to conform more closely to the POSIX standard by changing the behavior to match that specified by POSIX in areas where the Bash default differs.

When invoked as sh, Bash enters POSIX mode after reading the startup files.

The following list is what's changed when 'POSIX mode' is in effect:

1. When a command in the hash table no longer exists, Bash will research $PATH to find the new location. This is also available with 'shopt -s checkhash'.

2. The message printed by the job control code and builtins when a job exits with a non-zero status is 'Done(status)'.

3. The message printed by the job control code and builtins when a job is stopped is 'Stopped(*signame*)', where *signame* is, for example, SIGTSTP.

4. The bg builtin uses the required format to describe each job placed in the background, which does not include an indication of whether the job is the current or previous job.

5. Reserved words appearing in a context where reserved words are recognized do not undergo alias expansion.

6. The POSIX PS1 and PS2 expansions of '!' to the history number and '!!' to '!' are enabled, and parameter expansion is performed on the values of PS1 and PS2 regardless of the setting of the promptvars option.

7. The POSIX startup files are executed ($ENV) rather than the normal Bash files.

8. Tilde expansion is only performed on assignments preceding a command name, rather than on all assignment statements on the line.

9. The default history file is '~/.sh_history' (this is the default value of $HISTFILE).

10. The output of 'kill -l' prints all the signal names on a single line, separated by spaces, without the 'SIG' prefix.

11. The kill builtin does not accept signal names with a 'SIG' prefix.

12. Non-interactive shells exit if *filename* in . *filename* is not found.

13. Non-interactive shells exit if a syntax error in an arithmetic expansion results in an invalid expression.

14. Redirection operators do not perform filename expansion on the word in the redirection unless the shell is interactive.

15. Redirection operators do not perform word splitting on the word in the redirection.

16. Function names must be valid shell names. That is, they may not contain characters other than letters, digits, and underscores, and may not start with a digit. Declaring a function with an invalid name causes a fatal syntax error in non-interactive shells.

17. POSIX special builtins are found before shell functions during command lookup.

18. If a POSIX special builtin returns an error status, a non-interactive shell exits. The fatal errors are those listed in the POSIX standard, and include things like passing incorrect options, redirection errors, variable assignment errors for assignments preceding the command name, and so on.

19. If CDPATH is set, the cd builtin will not implicitly append the current directory to it. This means that cd will fail if no valid directory name can be constructed from any of the entries in $CDPATH, even if the a directory with the same name as the name given as an argument to cd exists in the current directory.

20. A non-interactive shell exits with an error status if a variable assignment error occurs when no command name follows the assignment statements. A variable assignment error occurs, for example, when trying to assign a value to a readonly variable.

21. A non-interactive shell exits with an error status if the iteration variable in a for statement or the selection variable in a select statement is a readonly variable.

22. Process substitution is not available.

23. Assignment statements preceding POSIX special builtins persist in the shell environment after the builtin completes.

24. Assignment statements preceding shell function calls persist in the shell environment after the function returns, as if a POSIX special builtin command had been executed.

25. The export and readonly builtin commands display their output in the format required by POSIX.

26. The trap builtin displays signal names without the leading SIG.

27. The trap builtin doesn't check the first argument for a possible signal specification and revert the signal handling to the original disposition

if it is, unless that argument consists solely of digits and is a valid signal number. If users want to reset the handler for a given signal to the original disposition, they should use '-' as the first argument.

28. The . and source builtins do not search the current directory for the filename argument if it is not found by searching PATH.

29. Subshells spawned to execute command substitutions inherit the value of the '-e' option from the parent shell. When not in POSIX mode, Bash clears the '-e' option in such subshells.

30. Alias expansion is always enabled, even in non-interactive shells.

31. When the alias builtin displays alias definitions, it does not display them with a leading 'alias ' unless the '-p' option is supplied.

32. When the set builtin is invoked without options, it does not display shell function names and definitions.

33. When the set builtin is invoked without options, it displays variable values without quotes, unless they contain shell metacharacters, even if the result contains nonprinting characters.

34. When the cd builtin is invoked in *logical* mode, and the pathname constructed from $PWD and the directory name supplied as an argument does not refer to an existing directory, cd will fail instead of falling back to *physical* mode.

35. When the pwd builtin is supplied the '-P' option, it resets $PWD to a pathname containing no symlinks.

36. The pwd builtin verifies that the value it prints is the same as the current directory, even if it is not asked to check the file system with the '-P' option.

37. When listing the history, the fc builtin does not include an indication of whether or not a history entry has been modified.

38. The default editor used by fc is ed.

39. The type and command builtins will not report a non-executable file as having been found, though the shell will attempt to execute such a file if it is the only so-named file found in $PATH.

40. The vi editing mode will invoke the vi editor directly when the 'v' command is run, instead of checking $FCEDIT and $EDITOR.

41. When the xpg_echo option is enabled, Bash does not attempt to interpret any arguments to echo as options. Each argument is displayed, after escape characters are converted.

There is other POSIX behavior that Bash does not implement by default even when in POSIX mode. Specifically:

1. The fc builtin checks $EDITOR as a program to edit history entries if FCEDIT is unset, rather than defaulting directly to ed. fc uses ed if EDITOR is unset.

2. As noted above, Bash requires the xpg_echo option to be enabled for the echo builtin to be fully conformant.

Bash can be configured to be POSIX-conformant by default, by specifying the '--enable-strict-posix-default' to configure when building (see Section 10.8 [Optional Features], page 154).

7 Job Control

This chapter discusses what job control is, how it works, and how Bash allows you to access its facilities.

7.1 Job Control Basics

Job control refers to the ability to selectively stop (suspend) the execution of processes and continue (resume) their execution at a later point. A user typically employs this facility via an interactive interface supplied jointly by the system's terminal driver and Bash.

The shell associates a *job* with each pipeline. It keeps a table of currently executing jobs, which may be listed with the jobs command. When Bash starts a job asynchronously, it prints a line that looks like:

    [1] 25647

indicating that this job is job number 1 and that the process ID of the last process in the pipeline associated with this job is 25647. All of the processes in a single pipeline are members of the same job. Bash uses the *job* abstraction as the basis for job control.

To facilitate the implementation of the user interface to job control, the operating system maintains the notion of a current terminal process group ID. Members of this process group (processes whose process group ID is equal to the current terminal process group ID) receive keyboard-generated signals such as SIGINT. These processes are said to be in the foreground. Background processes are those whose process group ID differs from the terminal's; such processes are immune to keyboard-generated signals. Only foreground processes are allowed to read from or write to the terminal. Background processes which attempt to read from (write to) the terminal are sent a SIGTTIN (SIGTTOU) signal by the terminal driver, which, unless caught, suspends the process.

If the operating system on which Bash is running supports job control, Bash contains facilities to use it. Typing the *suspend* character (typically '^Z', Control-Z) while a process is running causes that process to be stopped and returns control to Bash. Typing the *delayed suspend* character (typically '^Y', Control-Y) causes the process to be stopped when it attempts to read input from the terminal, and control to be returned to Bash. The user then manipulates the state of this job, using the bg command to continue it in the background, the fg command to continue it in the foreground, or the kill command to kill it. A '^Z' takes effect immediately, and has the additional side effect of causing pending output and typeahead to be discarded.

There are a number of ways to refer to a job in the shell. The character '%' introduces a job name.

Job number n may be referred to as '%n'. The symbols '%%' and '%+' refer to the shell's notion of the current job, which is the last job stopped while it was in the foreground or started in the background. A single '%' (with no accompanying job specification) also refers to the current job. The previous job may be referenced using '%-'. In output pertaining to jobs (e.g., the output of the jobs command), the current job is always flagged with a '+', and the previous job with a '-'.

A job may also be referred to using a prefix of the name used to start it, or using a substring that appears in its command line. For example, '%ce' refers to a stopped ce job. Using '%?ce', on the other hand, refers to any job containing the string 'ce' in its command line. If the prefix or substring matches more than one job, Bash reports an error.

Simply naming a job can be used to bring it into the foreground: '%1' is a synonym for 'fg %1', bringing job 1 from the background into the foreground. Similarly, '%1 &' resumes job 1 in the background, equivalent to 'bg %1'

The shell learns immediately whenever a job changes state. Normally, Bash waits until it is about to print a prompt before reporting changes in a job's status so as to not interrupt any other output. If the '-b' option to the set builtin is enabled, Bash reports such changes immediately (see Section 4.3 [The Set Builtin], page 66). Any trap on SIGCHLD is executed for each child process that exits.

If an attempt to exit Bash is made while jobs are stopped, the shell prints a message warning that there are stopped jobs. The jobs command may then be used to inspect their status. If a second attempt to exit is made without an intervening command, Bash does not print another warning, and the stopped jobs are terminated.

7.2 Job Control Builtins

bg

> bg [*jobspec* ...]
>
> Resume each suspended job *jobspec* in the background, as if it had been started with '&'. If *jobspec* is not supplied, the current job is used. The return status is zero unless it is run when job control is not enabled, or, when run with job control enabled, any *jobspec* was not found or specifies a job that was started without job control.

fg

fg [*jobspec*]

Resume the job *jobspec* in the foreground and make it the current job. If *jobspec* is not supplied, the current job is used. The return status is that of the command placed into the foreground, or non-zero if run when job control is disabled or, when run with job control enabled, *jobspec* does not specify a valid job or *jobspec* specifies a job that was started without job control.

jobs

jobs [-lnprs] [*jobspec*]
jobs -x *command* [*arguments*]

The first form lists the active jobs. The options have the following meanings:

-l   List process IDs in addition to the normal information.

-n   Display information only about jobs that have changed status since the user was last notified of their status.

-p   List only the process ID of the job's process group leader.

-r   Restrict output to running jobs.

-s   Restrict output to stopped jobs.

If *jobspec* is given, output is restricted to information about that job. If *jobspec* is not supplied, the status of all jobs is listed.

If the '-x' option is supplied, jobs replaces any *jobspec* found in *command* or *arguments* with the corresponding process group ID, and executes *command*, passing it *arguments*, returning its exit status.

kill

kill [-s *sigspec*] [-n *signum*] [-*sigspec*] *jobspec*
   or *pid*
kill -l [*exit_status*]

Send a signal specified by *sigspec* or *signum* to the process named by job specification *jobspec* or process ID *pid*. *sigspec* is either a case-insensitive signal name such as SIGINT (with or without the SIG prefix) or a signal number; *signum* is a signal number. If *sigspec* and *signum* are not present,

SIGTERM is used. The '-l' option lists the signal names. If any arguments are supplied when '-l' is given, the names of the signals corresponding to the arguments are listed, and the return status is zero. *exit_status* is a number specifying a signal number or the exit status of a process terminated by a signal. The return status is zero if at least one signal was successfully sent, or non-zero if an error occurs or an invalid option is encountered.

wait

> wait [*jobspec* or *pid* ...]
> Wait until the child process specified by each process ID *pid* or job specification *jobspec* exits and return the exit status of the last command waited for. If a job spec is given, all processes in the job are waited for. If no arguments are given, all currently active child processes are waited for, and the return status is zero. If neither *jobspec* nor *pid* specifies an active child process of the shell, the return status is 127.

disown

> disown [-ar] [-h] [*jobspec* ...]
> Without options, each *jobspec* is removed from the table of active jobs. If the '-h' option is given, the job is not removed from the table, but is marked so that SIGHUP is not sent to the job if the shell receives a SIGHUP. If *jobspec* is not present, and neither the '-a' nor '-r' option is supplied, the current job is used. If no *jobspec* is supplied, the '-a' option means to remove or mark all jobs; the '-r' option without a *jobspec* argument restricts operation to running jobs.

suspend

> suspend [-f]
> Suspend the execution of this shell until it receives a SIGCONT signal. The '-f' option means to suspend even if the shell is a login shell.

When job control is not active, the kill and wait builtins do not accept *jobspec* arguments. They must be supplied process IDs.

7.3 Job Control Variables

auto_resume

> This variable controls how the shell interacts with the user and job control. If this variable exists then single word sim-

ple commands without redirections are treated as candidates for resumption of an existing job. There is no ambiguity allowed; if there is more than one job beginning with the string typed, then the most recently accessed job will be selected. The name of a stopped job, in this context, is the command line used to start it. If this variable is set to the value 'exact', the string supplied must match the name of a stopped job exactly; if set to 'substring', the string supplied needs to match a substring of the name of a stopped job. The 'substring' value provides functionality analogous to the '%?' job ID (see Section 7.1 [Job Control Basics], page 107). If set to any other value, the supplied string must be a prefix of a stopped job's name; this provides functionality analogous to the '%' job ID.

8 Command Line Editing

This chapter describes the basic features of the GNU command line editing interface. Command line editing is provided by the Readline library, which is used by several different programs, including Bash.

8.1 Introduction to Line Editing

The following paragraphs describe the notation used to represent keystrokes.

The text C-k is read as 'Control-K' and describes the character produced when the (k) key is pressed while the Control key is depressed.

The text M-k is read as 'Meta-K' and describes the character produced when the Meta key (if you have one) is depressed, and the (k) key is pressed. The Meta key is labeled (ALT) on many keyboards. On keyboards with two keys labeled (ALT) (usually to either side of the space bar), the (ALT) on the left side is generally set to work as a Meta key. The (ALT) key on the right may also be configured to work as a Meta key or may be configured as some other modifier, such as a Compose key for typing accented characters.

If you do not have a Meta or (ALT) key, or another key working as a Meta key, the identical keystroke can be generated by typing (ESC) *first*, and then typing (k). Either process is known as *metafying* the (k) key.

The text M-C-k is read as 'Meta-Control-k' and describes the character produced by *metafying* C-k.

In addition, several keys have their own names. Specifically, (DEL), (ESC), (LFD), (SPC), (RET), and (TAB) all stand for themselves when seen in this text, or in an init file (see Section 8.3 [Readline Init File], page 117). If your keyboard lacks a (LFD) key, typing (C-j) will produce the desired character. The (RET) key may be labeled (Return) or (Enter) on some keyboards.

8.2 Readline Interaction

Often during an interactive session you type in a long line of text, only to notice that the first word on the line is misspelled. The Readline library gives you a set of commands for manipulating the text as you type it in, allowing you to just fix your typo, and not forcing you to retype the majority of the line. Using these editing commands, you move the cursor to the place that needs correction, and delete or insert the text of the corrections. Then, when you are satisfied with the line, you simply press (RET). You do not have to be at the end of the line to press (RET); the entire line is accepted regardless of the location of the cursor within the line.

8.2.1 Readline Bare Essentials

In order to enter characters into the line, simply type them. The typed character appears where the cursor was, and then the cursor moves one space to the right. If you mistype a character, you can use your erase character to back up and delete the mistyped character.

Sometimes you may mistype a character, and not notice the error until you have typed several other characters. In that case, you can type C-b to move the cursor to the left, and then correct your mistake. Afterwards, you can move the cursor to the right with C-f.

When you add text in the middle of a line, you will notice that characters to the right of the cursor are 'pushed over' to make room for the text that you have inserted. Likewise, when you delete text behind the cursor, characters to the right of the cursor are 'pulled back' to fill in the blank space created by the removal of the text. A list of the bare essentials for editing the text of an input line follows.

C-b   Move back one character.

C-f   Move forward one character.

(DEL) or (Backspace)
              Delete the character to the left of the cursor.

C-d   Delete the character underneath the cursor.

Printing characters
              Insert the character into the line at the cursor.

C-_ or C-x C-u
              Undo the last editing command. You can undo all the way
              back to an empty line.

(Depending on your configuration, the (Backspace) key be set to delete the character to the left of the cursor and the (DEL) key set to delete the character underneath the cursor, like C-d, rather than the character to the left of the cursor.)

8.2.2 Readline Movement Commands

The above table describes the most basic keystrokes that you need in order to do editing of the input line. For your convenience, many other commands have been added in addition to C-b, C-f, C-d, and (DEL). Here are some commands for moving more rapidly about the line.

C-a   Move to the start of the line.

C-e   Move to the end of the line.

M-f   Move forward a word, where a word is composed of letters
              and digits.

M-b   Move backward a word.

C-l   Clear the screen, reprinting the current line at the top.

Notice how C-f moves forward a character, while M-f moves forward
a word. It is a loose convention that control keystrokes operate on characters while meta keystrokes operate on words.

8.2.3 Readline Killing Commands

Killing text means to delete the text from the line, but to save it away
for later use, usually by *yanking* (re-inserting) it back into the line. ('Cut'
and 'paste' are more recent jargon for 'kill' and 'yank'.)

If the description for a command says that it 'kills' text, then you can
be sure that you can get the text back in a different (or the same) place
later.

When you use a kill command, the text is saved in a *kill-ring*. Any
number of consecutive kills save all of the killed text together, so that
when you yank it back, you get it all. The kill ring is not line specific; the
text that you killed on a previously typed line is available to be yanked
back later, when you are typing another line.

Here is the list of commands for killing text.

C-k   Kill the text from the current cursor position to the end of
              the line.

M-d   Kill from the cursor to the end of the current word, or, if be-
              tween words, to the end of the next word. Word boundaries
              are the same as those used by M-f.

M-DEL   Kill from the cursor the start of the current word, or, if
              between words, to the start of the previous word. Word
              boundaries are the same as those used by M-b.

C-w   Kill from the cursor to the previous whitespace. This is
              different than M-DEL because the word boundaries differ.

Here is how to *yank* the text back into the line. Yanking means to
copy the most-recently-killed text from the kill buffer.

C-y   Yank the most recently killed text back into the buffer at
              the cursor.

M-y   Rotate the kill-ring, and yank the new top. You can only do
           this if the prior command is *C-y* or *M-y*.

8.2.4 Readline Arguments

You can pass numeric arguments to Readline commands. Sometimes
the argument acts as a repeat count, other times it is the *sign* of the argument that is significant. If you pass a negative argument to a command
which normally acts in a forward direction, that command will act in a
backward direction. For example, to kill text back to the start of the line,
you might type 'M-- C-k'.

The general way to pass numeric arguments to a command is to type
meta digits before the command. If the first 'digit' typed is a minus sign
('-'), then the sign of the argument will be negative. Once you have typed
one meta digit to get the argument started, you can type the remainder of
the digits, and then the command. For example, to give the *C-d* command
an argument of 10, you could type 'M-1 0 C-d', which will delete the next
ten characters on the input line.

8.2.5 Searching for Commands in the History

Readline provides commands for searching through the command history (see Section 9.1 [Bash History Facilities], page 145) for lines containing a specified string. There are two search modes: *incremental* and
non-incremental.

Incremental searches begin before the user has finished typing the
search string. As each character of the search string is typed, Readline
displays the next entry from the history matching the string typed so
far. An incremental search requires only as many characters as needed
to find the desired history entry. To search backward in the history for
a particular string, type *C-r*. Typing *C-s* searches forward through the
history. The characters present in the value of the isearch-terminators
variable are used to terminate an incremental search. If that variable has
not been assigned a value, the (ESC) and *C-J* characters will terminate an
incremental search. *C-g* will abort an incremental search and restore the
original line. When the search is terminated, the history entry containing
the search string becomes the current line.

To find other matching entries in the history list, type *C-r* or *C-s*
as appropriate. This will search backward or forward in the history for
the next entry matching the search string typed so far. Any other key
sequence bound to a Readline command will terminate the search and
execute that command. For instance, a (RET) will terminate the search
and accept the line, thereby executing the command from the history list.

A movement command will terminate the search, make the last line found the current line, and begin editing.

Readline remembers the last incremental search string. If two *C-r*s are typed without any intervening characters defining a new search string, any remembered search string is used.

Non-incremental searches read the entire search string before starting to search for matching history lines. The search string may be typed by the user or be part of the contents of the current line.

8.3 Readline Init File

Although the Readline library comes with a set of Emacs-like keybindings installed by default, it is possible to use a different set of keybindings. Any user can customize programs that use Readline by putting commands in an *inputrc* file, conventionally in his home directory. The name of this file is taken from the value of the shell variable INPUTRC. If that variable is unset, the default is '~/.inputrc'. If that file does not exist or cannot be read, the ultimate default is '/etc/inputrc'.

When a program which uses the Readline library starts up, the init file is read, and the key bindings are set.

In addition, the C-x C-r command re-reads this init file, thus incorporating any changes that you might have made to it.

8.3.1 Readline Init File Syntax

There are only a few basic constructs allowed in the Readline init file. Blank lines are ignored. Lines beginning with a '#' are comments. Lines beginning with a '$' indicate conditional constructs (see Section 8.3.2 [Conditional Init Constructs], page 124). Other lines denote variable settings and key bindings.

Variable Settings

> You can modify the run-time behavior of Readline by altering the values of variables in Readline using the set command within the init file. The syntax is simple:
>
> set *variable value*
>
> Here, for example, is how to change from the default Emacs-like key binding to use vi line editing commands:
>
> set editing-mode vi
>
> Variable names and values, where appropriate, are recognized without regard to case. Unrecognized variable names are ignored.

Boolean variables (those that can be set to on or off) are set to on if the value is null or empty, *on* (case-insensitive), or 1. Any other value results in the variable being set to off.

The `bind -V` command lists the current Readline variable names and values. See Section 4.2 [Bash Builtins], page 51.

A great deal of run-time behavior is changeable with the following variables.

`bell-style`

Controls what happens when Readline wants to ring the terminal bell. If set to 'none', Readline never rings the bell. If set to 'visible', Readline uses a visible bell if one is available. If set to 'audible' (the default), Readline attempts to ring the terminal's bell.

`bind-tty-special-chars`

If set to 'on', Readline attempts to bind the control characters treated specially by the kernel's terminal driver to their Readline equivalents.

`comment-begin`

The string to insert at the beginning of the line when the insert-comment command is executed. The default value is "#".

`completion-ignore-case`

If set to 'on', Readline performs filename matching and completion in a case-insensitive fashion. The default value is 'off'.

`completion-query-items`

The number of possible completions that determines when the user is asked whether the list of possibilities should be displayed. If the number of possible completions is greater than this value, Readline will ask the user whether or not he wishes to view them; otherwise, they are simply listed. This variable must be set to an integer value greater than or equal to 0. A negative value means Readline should never ask. The default limit is 100.

`convert-meta`

If set to 'on', Readline will convert characters with the eighth bit set to an ASCII key sequence by stripping the eighth bit and prefixing an (ESC) character, converting them to a meta-prefixed key sequence. The default value is 'on'.

disable-completion

If set to 'On', Readline will inhibit word completion. Completion characters will be inserted into the line as if they had been mapped to self-insert. The default is 'off'.

editing-mode

The editing-mode variable controls which default set of key bindings is used. By default, Readline starts up in Emacs editing mode, where the keystrokes are most similar to Emacs. This variable can be set to either 'emacs' or 'vi'.

enable-keypad

When set to 'on', Readline will try to enable the application keypad when it is called. Some systems need this to enable the arrow keys. The default is 'off'.

expand-tilde

If set to 'on', tilde expansion is performed when Readline attempts word completion. The default is 'off'.

history-preserve-point

If set to 'on', the history code attempts to place point at the same location on each history line retrieved with previous-history or next-history. The default is 'off'.

horizontal-scroll-mode

This variable can be set to either 'on' or 'off'. Setting it to 'on' means that the text of the lines being edited will scroll horizontally on a single screen line when they are longer than the width of the screen, instead of wrapping onto a new screen line. By default, this variable is set to 'off'.

input-meta

If set to 'on', Readline will enable eight-bit input (it will not clear the eighth bit in the characters it reads), regardless of what the terminal claims it can support. The default value is 'off'. The name meta-flag is a synonym for this variable.

isearch-terminators
: The string of characters that should terminate an incremental search without subsequently executing the character as a command (see Section 8.2.5 [Searching], page 116). If this variable has not been given a value, the characters (ESC) and C-J will terminate an incremental search.

keymap
: Sets Readline's idea of the current keymap for key binding commands. Acceptable keymap names are emacs, emacs-standard, emacs-meta, emacs-ctlx, vi, vi-move, vi-command, and vi-insert. vi is equivalent to vi-command; emacs is equivalent to emacs-standard. The default value is emacs. The value of the editing-mode variable also affects the default keymap.

mark-directories
: If set to 'on', completed directory names have a slash appended. The default is 'on'.

mark-modified-lines
: This variable, when set to 'on', causes Readline to display an asterisk ('*') at the start of history lines which have been modified. This variable is 'off' by default.

mark-symlinked-directories
: If set to 'on', completed names which are symbolic links to directories have a slash appended (subject to the value of mark-directories). The default is 'off'.

match-hidden-files
: This variable, when set to 'on', causes Readline to match files whose names begin with a '.' (hidden files) when performing filename completion, unless the leading '.' is supplied by the user in the filename to be completed. This variable is 'on' by default.

output-meta

> If set to 'on', Readline will display characters with the eighth bit set directly rather than as a meta-prefixed escape sequence. The default is 'off'.

page-completions

> If set to 'on', Readline uses an internal more-like pager to display a screenful of possible completions at a time. This variable is 'on' by default.

print-completions-horizontally

> If set to 'on', Readline will display completions with matches sorted horizontally in alphabetical order, rather than down the screen. The default is 'off'.

show-all-if-ambiguous

> This alters the default behavior of the completion functions. If set to 'on', words which have more than one possible completion cause the matches to be listed immediately instead of ringing the bell. The default value is 'off'.

show-all-if-unmodified

> This alters the default behavior of the completion functions in a fashion similar to *show-all-if-ambiguous*. If set to 'on', words which have more than one possible completion without any possible partial completion (the possible completions don't share a common prefix) cause the matches to be listed immediately instead of ringing the bell. The default value is 'off'.

visible-stats

> If set to 'on', a character denoting a file's type is appended to the filename when listing possible completions. The default is 'off'.

Key Bindings

The syntax for controlling key bindings in the init file is simple. First you need to find the name of the command that you want to change. The following sections contain tables of the command name, the default keybinding, if any, and a short description of what the command does.

Once you know the name of the command, simply place on a line in the init file the name of the key you wish to bind the command to, a colon, and then the name of the command. There can be no space between the key name and the colon— that will be interpreted as part of the key name. The name of the key can be expressed in different ways, depending on what you find most comfortable.

In addition to command names, readline allows keys to be bound to a string that is inserted when the key is pressed (a *macro*).

The bind -p command displays Readline function names and bindings in a format that can put directly into an initialization file. See Section 4.2 [Bash Builtins], page 51.

keyname: *function-name* or *macro*

> *keyname* is the name of a key spelled out in English. For example:

```
Control-u: universal-argument
Meta-Rubout: backward-kill-word
Control-o: "> output"
```

> In the above example, *C-u* is bound to the function universal-argument, *M-DEL* is bound to the function backward-kill-word, and *C-o* is bound to run the macro expressed on the right hand side (that is, to insert the text '> output' into the line).

> A number of symbolic character names are recognized while processing this key binding syntax: *DEL, ESC, ESCAPE, LFD, NEWLINE, RET, RETURN, RUBOUT, SPACE, SPC*, and *TAB*.

"*keyseq*": *function-name* or *macro*

> *keyseq* differs from *keyname* above in that strings denoting an entire key sequence can be specified, by placing the key sequence in double quotes. Some GNU Emacs style key escapes can be used, as in the following example, but the special character names are not recognized.

```
"\C-u": universal-argument
"\C-x\C-r": re-read-init-file
"\e[11~": "Function Key 1"
```

In the above example, C-u is again bound to the function universal-argument (just as it was in the first example), 'C-x C-r' is bound to the function re-read-init-file, and '(ESC) (⦅) (1) (1) (⌒)' is bound to insert the text 'Function Key 1'.

The following GNU Emacs style escape sequences are available when specifying key sequences:

\C-	control prefix
\M-	meta prefix
\e	an escape character
\\	backslash
\"	(ⁿ), a double quotation mark
\'	(ᐟ), a single quote or apostrophe

In addition to the GNU Emacs style escape sequences, a second set of backslash escapes is available:

\a	alert (bell)
\b	backspace
\d	delete
\f	form feed
\n	newline
\r	carriage return
\t	horizontal tab
\v	vertical tab
\nnn	the eight-bit character whose value is the octal value nnn (one to three digits)
\xHH	the eight-bit character whose value is the hexadecimal value HH (one or two hex digits)

When entering the text of a macro, single or double quotes must be used to indicate a macro definition. Unquoted text is assumed to be a function name. In the macro body, the backslash escapes described above are expanded. Backslash will quote any other character in the macro text, including '"' and '''. For example, the following binding will make 'C-x \' insert a single '\' into the line:

```
"\C-x\\": "\\"
```

8.3.2 Conditional Init Constructs

Readline implements a facility similar in spirit to the conditional compilation features of the C preprocessor which allows key bindings and variable settings to be performed as the result of tests. There are four parser directives used.

$if   The $if construct allows bindings to be made based on the editing mode, the terminal being used, or the application using Readline. The text of the test extends to the end of the line; no characters are required to isolate it.

     mode   The mode= form of the $if directive is used to test whether Readline is in emacs or vi mode. This may be used in conjunction with the 'set keymap' command, for instance, to set bindings in the emacs-standard and emacs-ctlx keymaps only if Readline is starting out in emacs mode.

     term   The term= form may be used to include terminal-specific key bindings, perhaps to bind the key sequences output by the terminal's function keys. The word on the right side of the '=' is tested against both the full name of the terminal and the portion of the terminal name before the first '-'. This allows sun to match both sun and sun-cmd, for instance.

     application   The *application* construct is used to include application-specific settings. Each program using the Readline library sets the *application name*, and you can test for a particular value. This could be used to bind key sequences to functions useful for a specific program. For instance, the following command adds a key sequence that quotes the current or previous word in Bash:

```
$if Bash
# Quote the current or previous word
"\C-xq": "\eb\"\ef\""
$endif
```

$endif   This command, as seen in the previous example, terminates an $if command.

$else   Commands in this branch of the $if directive are executed
              if the test fails.

$include   This directive takes a single filename as an argument and
              reads commands and bindings from that file. For example,
              the following directive reads from '/etc/inputrc':

                    $include /etc/inputrc

8.3.3 Sample Init File

Here is an example of an *inputrc* file. This illustrates key binding,
variable assignment, and conditional syntax.

```
# This file controls the behaviour of line input editing
# for programs that use the GNU Readline library.
# Existing programs include FTP, Bash, and GDB.
#
# You can re-read the inputrc file with C-x C-r.
# Lines beginning with '#' are comments.
#
# First, include any systemwide bindings and variable
# assignments from /etc/Inputrc
$include /etc/Inputrc


#
# Set various bindings for emacs mode.

set editing-mode emacs

$if mode=emacs

# Text after the function name is ignored
Meta-Control-h:  backward-kill-word

#
# Arrow keys in keypad mode
#
#"\M-OD":        backward-char
#"\M-OC":        forward-char
#"\M-OA":        previous-history
#"\M-OB":        next-history
#
# Arrow keys in ANSI mode
```

```
#
"\M-[D":          backward-char
"\M-[C":          forward-char
"\M-[A":          previous-history
"\M-[B":          next-history
#
# Arrow keys in 8 bit keypad mode
#
#"\M-\C-OD":      backward-char
#"\M-\C-OC":      forward-char
#"\M-\C-OA":      previous-history
#"\M-\C-OB":      next-history
#
# Arrow keys in 8 bit ANSI mode
#
#"\M-\C-[D":      backward-char
#"\M-\C-[C":      forward-char
#"\M-\C-[A":      previous-history
#"\M-\C-[B":      next-history

C-q: quoted-insert

$endif

# An old-style binding.  This happens to be the default.
TAB: complete

# Macros that are convenient for shell interaction
$if Bash
# edit the path
"\C-xp": "PATH=${PATH}\e\C-e\C-a\ef\C-f"
# prepare to type a quoted word --
# insert open and close double quotes
# and move to just after the open quote
"\C-x\"": "\"\"\C-b"
# insert a backslash (testing backslash escapes
# in sequences and macros)
"\C-x\\": "\\"
# Quote the current or previous word
"\C-xq": "\eb\"\ef\""
# Add a binding to refresh the line, which is unbound
```

```
"\C-xr": redraw-current-line
# Edit variable on current line.
"\M-\C-v": "\C-a\C-k$\C-y\M-\C-e\C-a\C-y="
$endif


# use a visible bell if one is available
set bell-style visible

# don't strip characters to 7 bits when reading
set input-meta on

# allow iso-latin1 characters to be inserted rather
# than converted to prefix-meta sequences
set convert-meta off

# display characters with the eighth bit set directly
# rather than as meta-prefixed characters
set output-meta on

# if there are more than 150 possible completions for
# a word, ask if the user wants to see all of them
set completion-query-items 150

# For FTP
$if Ftp
"\C-xg": "get \M-?"
"\C-xt": "put \M-?"
"\M-.": yank-last-arg
$endif
```

8.4 Bindable Readline Commands

This section describes Readline commands that may be bound to key sequences. You can list your key bindings by executing bind -P or, for a more terse format, suitable for an *inputrc* file, bind -p. (See Section 4.2 [Bash Builtins], page 51.) Command names without an accompanying key sequence are unbound by default.

In the following descriptions, *point* refers to the current cursor position, and *mark* refers to a cursor position saved by the set-mark command. The text between the point and mark is referred to as the *region*.

8.4.1 Commands For Moving

beginning-of-line (C-a)
>   Move to the start of the current line.

end-of-line (C-e)
>   Move to the end of the line.

forward-char (C-f)
>   Move forward a character.

backward-char (C-b)
>   Move back a character.

forward-word (M-f)
>   Move forward to the end of the next word. Words are com-
>   posed of letters and digits.

backward-word (M-b)
>   Move back to the start of the current or previous word.
>   Words are composed of letters and digits.

clear-screen (C-l)
>   Clear the screen and redraw the current line, leaving the
>   current line at the top of the screen.

redraw-current-line ()
>   Refresh the current line. By default, this is unbound.

8.4.2 Commands For Manipulating The History

accept-line (Newline or Return)
>   Accept the line regardless of where the cursor is. If this
>   line is non-empty, add it to the history list according to the
>   setting of the HISTCONTROL and HISTIGNORE variables. If
>   this line is a modified history line, then restore the history
>   line to its original state.

previous-history (C-p)
>   Move 'back' through the history list, fetching the previous
>   command.

next-history (C-n)
>   Move 'forward' through the history list, fetching the next
>   command.

`beginning-of-history (M-<)`
>   Move to the first line in the history.

`end-of-history (M->)`
>   Move to the end of the input history, i.e., the line currently being entered.

`reverse-search-history (C-r)`
>   Search backward starting at the current line and moving 'up' through the history as necessary. This is an incremental search.

`forward-search-history (C-s)`
>   Search forward starting at the current line and moving 'down' through the the history as necessary. This is an incremental search.

`non-incremental-reverse-search-history (M-p)`
>   Search backward starting at the current line and moving 'up' through the history as necessary using a non-incremental search for a string supplied by the user.

`non-incremental-forward-search-history (M-n)`
>   Search forward starting at the current line and moving 'down' through the the history as necessary using a non-incremental search for a string supplied by the user.

`history-search-forward ()`
>   Search forward through the history for the string of characters between the start of the current line and the point. This is a non-incremental search. By default, this command is unbound.

`history-search-backward ()`
>   Search backward through the history for the string of characters between the start of the current line and the point. This is a non-incremental search. By default, this command is unbound.

`yank-nth-arg (M-C-y)`
>   Insert the first argument to the previous command (usually the second word on the previous line) at point. With an argument n, insert the nth word from the previous command (the words in the previous command begin with word 0). A negative argument inserts the nth word from the end of the previous command. Once the argument n is computed, the

argument is extracted as if the '!*n*' history expansion had
been specified.

yank-last-arg (M-. or M-_)
> Insert last argument to the previous command (the last word
> of the previous history entry). With an argument, behave
> exactly like yank-nth-arg. Successive calls to yank-last-
> arg move back through the history list, inserting the last
> argument of each line in turn. The history expansion fa-
> cilities are used to extract the last argument, as if the '!$'
> history expansion had been specified.

8.4.3 Commands For Changing Text

delete-char (C-d)
> Delete the character at point. If point is at the beginning
> of the line, there are no characters in the line, and the last
> character typed was not bound to delete-char, then return
> EOF.

backward-delete-char (Rubout)
> Delete the character behind the cursor. A numeric argument
> means to kill the characters instead of deleting them.

forward-backward-delete-char ()
> Delete the character under the cursor, unless the cursor is at
> the end of the line, in which case the character behind the
> cursor is deleted. By default, this is not bound to a key.

quoted-insert (C-q or C-v)
> Add the next character typed to the line verbatim. This is
> how to insert key sequences like *C-q*, for example.

self-insert (a, b, A, 1, !, ...)
> Insert yourself.

transpose-chars (C-t)
> Drag the character before the cursor forward over the char-
> acter at the cursor, moving the cursor forward as well. If the
> insertion point is at the end of the line, then this transposes
> the last two characters of the line. Negative arguments have
> no effect.

transpose-words (M-t)
> Drag the word before point past the word after point, moving
> point past that word as well. If the insertion point is at the

end of the line, this transposes the last two words on the line.

upcase-word (M-u)

Uppercase the current (or following) word. With a negative argument, uppercase the previous word, but do not move the cursor.

downcase-word (M-l)

Lowercase the current (or following) word. With a negative argument, lowercase the previous word, but do not move the cursor.

capitalize-word (M-c)

Capitalize the current (or following) word. With a negative argument, capitalize the previous word, but do not move the cursor.

overwrite-mode ()

Toggle overwrite mode. With an explicit positive numeric argument, switches to overwrite mode. With an explicit non-positive numeric argument, switches to insert mode. This command affects only emacs mode; vi mode does overwrite differently. Each call to readline() starts in insert mode.

In overwrite mode, characters bound to self-insert replace the text at point rather than pushing the text to the right. Characters bound to backward-delete-char replace the character before point with a space.

By default, this command is unbound.

8.4.4 Killing And Yanking

kill-line (C-k)

Kill the text from point to the end of the line.

backward-kill-line (C-x Rubout)

Kill backward to the beginning of the line.

unix-line-discard (C-u)

Kill backward from the cursor to the beginning of the current line.

kill-whole-line ()

Kill all characters on the current line, no matter where point is. By default, this is unbound.

`kill-word (M-d)`
> Kill from point to the end of the current word, or if between words, to the end of the next word. Word boundaries are the same as `forward-word`.

`backward-kill-word (M-`DEL`)`
> Kill the word behind point. Word boundaries are the same as `backward-word`.

`unix-word-rubout (C-w)`
> Kill the word behind point, using white space as a word boundary. The killed text is saved on the kill-ring.

`unix-filename-rubout ()`
> Kill the word behind point, using white space and the slash character as the word boundaries. The killed text is saved on the kill-ring.

`delete-horizontal-space ()`
> Delete all spaces and tabs around point. By default, this is unbound.

`kill-region ()`
> Kill the text in the current region. By default, this command is unbound.

`copy-region-as-kill ()`
> Copy the text in the region to the kill buffer, so it can be yanked right away. By default, this command is unbound.

`copy-backward-word ()`
> Copy the word before point to the kill buffer. The word boundaries are the same as `backward-word`. By default, this command is unbound.

`copy-forward-word ()`
> Copy the word following point to the kill buffer. The word boundaries are the same as `forward-word`. By default, this command is unbound.

`yank (C-y)`   Yank the top of the kill ring into the buffer at point.

`yank-pop (M-y)`
> Rotate the kill-ring, and yank the new top. You can only do this if the prior command is yank or yank-pop.

8.4.5 Specifying Numeric Arguments

digit-argument (*M-0*, *M-1*, ... *M--*)

Add this digit to the argument already accumulating, or start a new argument. *M--* starts a negative argument.

universal-argument ()

This is another way to specify an argument. If this command is followed by one or more digits, optionally with a leading minus sign, those digits define the argument. If the command is followed by digits, executing universal-argument again ends the numeric argument, but is otherwise ignored. As a special case, if this command is immediately followed by a character that is neither a digit or minus sign, the argument count for the next command is multiplied by four. The argument count is initially one, so executing this function the first time makes the argument count four, a second time makes the argument count sixteen, and so on. By default, this is not bound to a key.

8.4.6 Letting Readline Type For You

complete ((TAB))

Attempt to perform completion on the text before point. The actual completion performed is application-specific. Bash attempts completion treating the text as a variable (if the text begins with '$'), username (if the text begins with '~'), hostname (if the text begins with '@'), or command (including aliases and functions) in turn. If none of these produces a match, filename completion is attempted.

possible-completions (M-?)

List the possible completions of the text before point.

insert-completions (M-*)

Insert all completions of the text before point that would have been generated by possible-completions.

menu-complete ()

Similar to complete, but replaces the word to be completed with a single match from the list of possible completions. Repeated execution of menu-complete steps through the list of possible completions, inserting each match in turn. At the end of the list of completions, the bell is rung (subject

to the setting of bell-style) and the original text is restored. An argument of *n* moves *n* positions forward in the
list of matches; a negative argument may be used to move
backward through the list. This command is intended to be
bound to (TAB), but is unbound by default.

delete-char-or-list ()
> Deletes the character under the cursor if not at the beginning
> or end of the line (like delete-char). If at the end of the
> line, behaves identically to possible-completions. This
> command is unbound by default.

complete-filename (M-/)
> Attempt filename completion on the text before point.

possible-filename-completions (C-x /)
> List the possible completions of the text before point, treat-
> ing it as a filename.

complete-username (M-~)
> Attempt completion on the text before point, treating it as
> a username.

possible-username-completions (C-x ~)
> List the possible completions of the text before point, treat-
> ing it as a username.

complete-variable (M-$)
> Attempt completion on the text before point, treating it as
> a shell variable.

possible-variable-completions (C-x $)
> List the possible completions of the text before point, treat-
> ing it as a shell variable.

complete-hostname (M-@)
> Attempt completion on the text before point, treating it as
> a hostname.

possible-hostname-completions (C-x @)
> List the possible completions of the text before point, treat-
> ing it as a hostname.

complete-command (M-!)
> Attempt completion on the text before point, treating it as a
> command name. Command completion attempts to match
> the text against aliases, reserved words, shell functions, shell
> builtins, and finally executable filenames, in that order.

possible-command-completions (C-x !)
>   List the possible completions of the text before point, treat-
>   ing it as a command name.

dynamic-complete-history (M-TAB)
>   Attempt completion on the text before point, comparing the
>   text against lines from the history list for possible completion
>   matches.

complete-into-braces (M-{)
>   Perform filename completion and insert the list of possible
>   completions enclosed within braces so the list is available to
>   the shell (see Section 3.5.1 [Brace Expansion], page 23).

8.4.7 Keyboard Macros

start-kbd-macro (C-x ()
>   Begin saving the characters typed into the current keyboard
>   macro.

end-kbd-macro (C-x))
>   Stop saving the characters typed into the current keyboard
>   macro and save the definition.

call-last-kbd-macro (C-x e)
>   Re-execute the last keyboard macro defined, by making the
>   characters in the macro appear as if typed at the keyboard.

8.4.8 Some Miscellaneous Commands

re-read-init-file (C-x C-r)
>   Read in the contents of the *inputrc* file, and incorporate any
>   bindings or variable assignments found there.

abort (C-g)
>   Abort the current editing command and ring the terminal's
>   bell (subject to the setting of bell-style).

do-uppercase-version (M-a, M-b, M-x, ...)
>   If the metafied character x is lowercase, run the command
>   that is bound to the corresponding uppercase character.

prefix-meta (ESC)
>   Metafy the next character typed. This is for keyboards with-
>   out a meta key. Typing 'ESC f' is equivalent to typing M-f.

undo (C-_ or C-x C-u)
>   Incremental undo, separately remembered for each line.

revert-line (M-r)
>   Undo all changes made to this line. This is like executing the
>   undo command enough times to get back to the beginning.

tilde-expand (M-&)
>   Perform tilde expansion on the current word.

set-mark (C-@)
>   Set the mark to the point. If a numeric argument is supplied,
>   the mark is set to that position.

exchange-point-and-mark (C-x C-x)
>   Swap the point with the mark. The current cursor position
>   is set to the saved position, and the old cursor position is
>   saved as the mark.

character-search (C-])
>   A character is read and point is moved to the next occurrence
>   of that character. A negative count searches for previous
>   occurrences.

character-search-backward (M-C-])
>   A character is read and point is moved to the previous oc-
>   currence of that character. A negative count searches for
>   subsequent occurrences.

insert-comment (M-#)
>   Without a numeric argument, the value of the comment-
>   begin variable is inserted at the beginning of the current
>   line. If a numeric argument is supplied, this command acts
>   as a toggle: if the characters at the beginning of the line do
>   not match the value of comment-begin, the value is inserted,
>   otherwise the characters in comment-begin are deleted from
>   the beginning of the line. In either case, the line is ac-
>   cepted as if a newline had been typed. The default value
>   of comment-begin causes this command to make the cur-
>   rent line a shell comment. If a numeric argument causes the
>   comment character to be removed, the line will be executed
>   by the shell.

dump-functions ()
>   Print all of the functions and their key bindings to the Read-
>   line output stream. If a numeric argument is supplied, the

output is formatted in such a way that it can be made part of an *inputrc* file. This command is unbound by default.

dump-variables ()

> Print all of the settable variables and their values to the Readline output stream. If a numeric argument is supplied, the output is formatted in such a way that it can be made part of an *inputrc* file. This command is unbound by default.

dump-macros ()

> Print all of the Readline key sequences bound to macros and the strings they output. If a numeric argument is supplied, the output is formatted in such a way that it can be made part of an *inputrc* file. This command is unbound by default.

glob-complete-word (M-g)

> The word before point is treated as a pattern for pathname expansion, with an asterisk implicitly appended. This pattern is used to generate a list of matching file names for possible completions.

glob-expand-word (C-x *)

> The word before point is treated as a pattern for pathname expansion, and the list of matching file names is inserted, replacing the word. If a numeric argument is supplied, a '*' is appended before pathname expansion.

glob-list-expansions (C-x g)

> The list of expansions that would have been generated by glob-expand-word is displayed, and the line is redrawn. If a numeric argument is supplied, a '*' is appended before pathname expansion.

display-shell-version (C-x C-v)

> Display version information about the current instance of Bash.

shell-expand-line (M-C-e)

> Expand the line as the shell does. This performs alias and history expansion as well as all of the shell word expansions (see Section 3.5 [Shell Expansions], page 22).

history-expand-line (M-^)

> Perform history expansion on the current line.

magic-space ()
> Perform history expansion on the current line and insert a
> space (see Section 9.3 [History Interaction], page 147).

alias-expand-line ()
> Perform alias expansion on the current line (see Section 6.6
> [Aliases], page 95).

history-and-alias-expand-line ()
> Perform history and alias expansion on the current line.

insert-last-argument (M-. or M-_)
> A synonym for yank-last-arg.

operate-and-get-next (C-o)
> Accept the current line for execution and fetch the next line
> relative to the current line from the history for editing. Any
> argument is ignored.

edit-and-execute-command (C-xC-e)
> Invoke an editor on the current command line, and exe-
> cute the result as shell commands. Bash attempts to invoke
> $VISUAL, $EDITOR, and emacs as the editor, in that order.

8.5 Readline vi Mode

While the Readline library does not have a full set of vi editing functions, it does contain enough to allow simple editing of the line. The
Readline vi mode behaves as specified in the POSIX 1003.2 standard.

In order to switch interactively between emacs and vi editing modes,
use the 'set -o emacs' and 'set -o vi' commands (see Section 4.3 [The
Set Builtin], page 66). The Readline default is emacs mode.

When you enter a line in vi mode, you are already placed in 'insertion'
mode, as if you had typed an 'i'. Pressing (ESC) switches you into 'command' mode, where you can edit the text of the line with the standard vi
movement keys, move to previous history lines with 'k' and subsequent
lines with 'j', and so forth.

8.6 Programmable Completion

When word completion is attempted for an argument to a command for
which a completion specification (a *compspec*) has been defined using the
complete builtin (see Section 8.7 [Programmable Completion Builtins],
page 141), the programmable completion facilities are invoked.

First, the command name is identified. If a compspec has been defined for that command, the compspec is used to generate the list of possible completions for the word. If the command word is a full pathname, a compspec for the full pathname is searched for first. If no compspec is found for the full pathname, an attempt is made to find a compspec for the portion following the final slash.

Once a compspec has been found, it is used to generate the list of matching words. If a compspec is not found, the default Bash completion described above (see Section 8.4.6 [Commands For Completion], page 133) is performed.

First, the actions specified by the compspec are used. Only matches which are prefixed by the word being completed are returned. When the '-f' or '-d' option is used for filename or directory name completion, the shell variable FIGNORE is used to filter the matches. See Section 5.2 [Bash Variables], page 74, for a description of FIGNORE.

Any completions specified by a filename expansion pattern to the '-G' option are generated next. The words generated by the pattern need not match the word being completed. The GLOBIGNORE shell variable is not used to filter the matches, but the FIGNORE shell variable is used.

Next, the string specified as the argument to the '-W' option is considered. The string is first split using the characters in the IFS special variable as delimiters. Shell quoting is honored. Each word is then expanded using brace expansion, tilde expansion, parameter and variable expansion, command substitution, and arithmetic expansion, as described above (see Section 3.5 [Shell Expansions], page 22). The results are split using the rules described above (see Section 3.5.7 [Word Splitting], page 29). The results of the expansion are prefix-matched against the word being completed, and the matching words become the possible completions.

After these matches have been generated, any shell function or command specified with the '-F' and '-C' options is invoked. When the command or function is invoked, the COMP_LINE and COMP_POINT variables are assigned values as described above (see Section 5.2 [Bash Variables], page 74). If a shell function is being invoked, the COMP_WORDS and COMP_CWORD variables are also set. When the function or command is invoked, the first argument is the name of the command whose arguments are being completed, the second argument is the word being completed, and the third argument is the word preceding the word being completed on the current command line. No filtering of the generated completions against the word being completed is performed; the function or command has complete freedom in generating the matches.

Any function specified with '-F' is invoked first. The function may use any of the shell facilities, including the compgen builtin described below (see Section 8.7 [Programmable Completion Builtins], page 141), to generate the matches. It must put the possible completions in the COMPREPLY array variable.

Next, any command specified with the '-C' option is invoked in an environment equivalent to command substitution. It should print a list of completions, one per line, to the standard output. Backslash may be used to escape a newline, if necessary.

After all of the possible completions are generated, any filter specified with the '-X' option is applied to the list. The filter is a pattern as used for pathname expansion; an ampersand '&' in the pattern is replaced with the text of the word being completed. A literal '&' may be escaped with a backslash; the backslash is removed before attempting a match. Any completion that matches the pattern will be removed from the list. A leading '!' negates the pattern; in this case any completion not matching the pattern will be removed.

Finally, any prefix and suffix specified with the '-P' and '-S' options are added to each member of the completion list, and the result is returned to the Readline completion code as the list of possible completions.

If the previously-applied actions do not generate any matches, and the '-o dirnames' option was supplied to complete when the compspec was defined, directory name completion is attempted.

If the '-o plusdirs' option was supplied to complete when the compspec was defined, directory name completion is attempted and any matches are added to the results of the other actions.

By default, if a compspec is found, whatever it generates is returned to the completion code as the full set of possible completions. The default Bash completions are not attempted, and the Readline default of filename completion is disabled. If the '-o bashdefault' option was supplied to complete when the compspec was defined, the default Bash completions are attempted if the compspec generates no matches. If the '-o default' option was supplied to complete when the compspec was defined, Readline's default completion will be performed if the compspec (and, if attempted, the default Bash completions) generate no matches.

When a compspec indicates that directory name completion is desired, the programmable completion functions force Readline to append a slash to completed names which are symbolic links to directories, subject to the value of the *mark-directories* Readline variable, regardless of the setting of the *mark-symlinked-directories* Readline variable.

8.7 Programmable Completion Builtins

Two builtin commands are available to manipulate the programmable completion facilities.

compgen

> compgen [*option*] [*word*]
>
> Generate possible completion matches for *word* according to the *options*, which may be any option accepted by the complete builtin with the exception of '-p' and '-r', and write the matches to the standard output. When using the '-F' or '-C' options, the various shell variables set by the programmable completion facilities, while available, will not have useful values.
>
> The matches will be generated in the same way as if the programmable completion code had generated them directly from a completion specification with the same flags. If *word* is specified, only those completions matching *word* will be displayed.
>
> The return value is true unless an invalid option is supplied, or no matches were generated.

complete

> complete [-abcdefgjksuv] [-o *comp-option*]
> [-A *action*] [-G *globpat*] [-W *wordlist*]
> [-P *prefix*] [-S *suffix*] [-X *filterpat*] [-F *function*]
> [-C *command*] *name* [*name* ...]
> complete -pr [*name* ...]
>
> Specify how arguments to each *name* should be completed. If the '-p' option is supplied, or if no options are supplied, existing completion specifications are printed in a way that allows them to be reused as input. The '-r' option removes a completion specification for each *name*, or, if no *names* are supplied, all completion specifications.
>
> The process of applying these completion specifications when word completion is attempted is described above (see Section 8.6 [Programmable Completion], page 138).
>
> Other options, if specified, have the following meanings. The arguments to the '-G', '-W', and '-X' options (and, if necessary, the '-P' and '-S' options) should be quoted to protect them from expansion before the complete builtin is invoked.

-o *comp-option*

> The *comp-option* controls several aspects of the compspec's behavior beyond the simple generation of completions. *comp-option* may be one of:

> `bashdefault`
>> Perform the rest of the default Bash completions if the compspec generates no matches.

> `default`
>> Use Readline's default filename completion if the compspec generates no matches.

> `dirnames`
>> Perform directory name completion if the compspec generates no matches.

> `filenames`
>> Tell Readline that the compspec generates filenames, so it can perform any filename-specific processing (like adding a slash to directory names or suppressing trailing spaces). This option is intended to be used with shell functions specified with '-F'.

> `nospace`
>> Tell Readline not to append a space (the default) to words completed at the end of the line.

> `plusdirs`
>> After any matches defined by the compspec are generated, directory name completion is attempted and any matches are added to the results of the other actions.

-A *action*

> The *action* may be one of the following to generate a list of possible completions:

> `alias`
>> Alias names. May also be specified as '-a'.

> `arrayvar`
>> Array variable names.

> `binding`
>> Readline key binding names (see Section 8.4 [Bindable Readline Commands], page 127).

builtin	Names of shell builtin commands. May also be specified as '-b'.
command	Command names. May also be specified as '-c'.
directory	Directory names. May also be specified as '-d'.
disabled	Names of disabled shell builtins.
enabled	Names of enabled shell builtins.
export	Names of exported shell variables. May also be specified as '-e'.
file	File names. May also be specified as '-f'.
function	Names of shell functions.
group	Group names. May also be specified as '-g'.
helptopic	Help topics as accepted by the help builtin (see Section 4.2 [Bash Builtins], page 51).
hostname	Hostnames, as taken from the file specified by the HOSTFILE shell variable (see Section 5.2 [Bash Variables], page 74).
job	Job names, if job control is active. May also be specified as '-j'.
keyword	Shell reserved words. May also be specified as '-k'.
running	Names of running jobs, if job control is active.
service	Service names. May also be specified as '-s'.
setopt	Valid arguments for the '-o' option to the set builtin (see Section 4.3 [The Set Builtin], page 66).
shopt	Shell option names as accepted by the shopt builtin (see Section 4.2 [Bash Builtins], page 51).

signal   Signal names.

stopped   Names of stopped jobs, if job con-
           trol is active.

user   User names. May also be speci-
           fied as '-u'.

variable   Names of all shell variables. May
           also be specified as '-v'.

-G *globpat*   The filename expansion pattern *globpat* is ex-
               panded to generate the possible completions.

-W *wordlist* The *wordlist* is split using the characters in the
               IFS special variable as delimiters, and each re-
               sultant word is expanded. The possible com-
               pletions are the members of the resultant list
               which match the word being completed.

-C *command*

               command is executed in a subshell environ-
               ment, and its output is used as the possible
               completions.

-F *function* The shell function *function* is executed in the
               current shell environment. When it finishes,
               the possible completions are retrieved from the
               value of the COMPREPLY array variable.

-X *filterpat* *filterpat* is a pattern as used for filename expan-
               sion. It is applied to the list of possible comple-
               tions generated by the preceding options and
               arguments, and each completion matching *fil-
               terpat* is removed from the list. A leading '!' in
               filterpat negates the pattern; in this case, any
               completion not matching *filterpat* is removed.

-P *prefix*   *prefix* is added at the beginning of each possible
               completion after all other options have been
               applied.

-S *suffix*   *suffix* is appended to each possible completion
               after all other options have been applied.

The return value is true unless an invalid option is supplied,
an option other than '-p' or '-r' is supplied without a *name*
argument, an attempt is made to remove a completion specification for a *name* for which no specification exists, or an
error occurs adding a completion specification.

9 Using History Interactively

This chapter describes how to use the GNU History Library interactively, from a user's standpoint. It should be considered a user's guide. For information on using the GNU History Library in other programs, see the GNU Readline Library Manual.

9.1 Bash History Facilities

When the '-o history' option to the set builtin is enabled (see Section 4.3 [The Set Builtin], page 66), the shell provides access to the *command history*, the list of commands previously typed. The value of the HISTSIZE shell variable is used as the number of commands to save in a history list. The text of the last $HISTSIZE commands (default 500) is saved. The shell stores each command in the history list prior to parameter and variable expansion but after history expansion is performed, subject to the values of the shell variables HISTIGNORE and HISTCONTROL.

When the shell starts up, the history is initialized from the file named by the HISTFILE variable (default '~/.bash_history'). The file named by the value of HISTFILE is truncated, if necessary, to contain no more than the number of lines specified by the value of the HISTFILESIZE variable. When an interactive shell exits, the last $HISTSIZE lines are copied from the history list to the file named by $HISTFILE. If the histappend shell option is set (see Section 4.2 [Bash Builtins], page 51), the lines are appended to the history file, otherwise the history file is overwritten. If HISTFILE is unset, or if the history file is unwritable, the history is not saved. After saving the history, the history file is truncated to contain no more than $HISTFILESIZE lines. If HISTFILESIZE is not set, no truncation is performed.

If the HISTTIMEFORMAT is set, the time stamp information associated with each history entry is written to the history file.

The builtin command fc may be used to list or edit and re-execute a portion of the history list. The history builtin may be used to display or modify the history list and manipulate the history file. When using command-line editing, search commands are available in each editing mode that provide access to the history list (see Section 8.4.2 [Commands For History], page 128).

The shell allows control over which commands are saved on the history list. The HISTCONTROL and HISTIGNORE variables may be set to cause the shell to save only a subset of the commands entered. The cmdhist shell option, if enabled, causes the shell to attempt to save each line of a multi-line command in the same history entry, adding semicolons where necessary to preserve syntactic correctness. The lithist shell option causes the shell to save the command with embedded newlines instead of semicolons. The shopt builtin is used to set these options. See Section 4.2 [Bash Builtins], page 51, for a description of shopt.

9.2 Bash History Builtins

Bash provides two builtin commands which manipulate the history list and history file.

fc

> ```
> fc [-e ename] [-nlr] [first] [last]
> fc -s [pat=rep] [command]
> ```
>
> Fix Command. In the first form, a range of commands from *first* to *last* is selected from the history list. Both *first* and *last* may be specified as a string (to locate the most recent command beginning with that string) or as a number (an index into the history list, where a negative number is used as an offset from the current command number). If *last* is not specified it is set to *first*. If *first* is not specified it is set to the previous command for editing and −16 for listing. If the '-l' flag is given, the commands are listed on standard output. The '-n' flag suppresses the command numbers when listing. The '-r' flag reverses the order of the listing. Otherwise, the editor given by *ename* is invoked on a file containing those commands. If *ename* is not given, the value of the following variable expansion is used: ${FCEDIT:-${EDITOR:-vi}}. This says to use the value of the FCEDIT variable if set, or the value of the EDITOR variable if that is set, or vi if neither is set. When editing is complete, the edited commands are echoed and executed.
>
> In the second form, *command* is re-executed after each instance of *pat* in the selected command is replaced by *rep*.
>
> A useful alias to use with the fc command is r='fc -s', so that typing 'r cc' runs the last command beginning with cc and typing 'r' re-executes the last command (see Section 6.6 [Aliases], page 95).

history

> ```
> history [n]
> history -c
> history -d offset
> ```

```
history [-anrw] [filename]
history -ps arg
```

With no options, display the history list with line numbers. Lines prefixed with a '*' have been modified. An argument of n lists only the last n lines. If the shell variable HISTTIMEFORMAT is set and not null, it is used as a format string for *strftime* to display the time stamp associated with each displayed history entry. No intervening blank is printed between the formatted time stamp and the history line.

Options, if supplied, have the following meanings:

-c   Clear the history list. This may be combined with the other options to replace the history list completely.

-d *offset*   Delete the history entry at position *offset*. *offset* should be specified as it appears when the history is displayed.

-a   Append the new history lines (history lines entered since the beginning of the current Bash session) to the history file.

-n   Append the history lines not already read from the history file to the current history list. These are lines appended to the history file since the beginning of the current Bash session.

-r   Read the current history file and append its contents to the history list.

-w   Write out the current history to the history file.

-p   Perform history substitution on the *args* and display the result on the standard output, without storing the results in the history list.

-s   The *args* are added to the end of the history list as a single entry.

When any of the '-w', '-r', '-a', or '-n' options is used, if *filename* is given, then it is used as the history file. If not, then the value of the HISTFILE variable is used.

9.3 History Expansion

The History library provides a history expansion feature that is similar to the history expansion provided by csh. This section describes the syntax used to manipulate the history information.

History expansions introduce words from the history list into the input stream, making it easy to repeat commands, insert the arguments to a previous command into the current input line, or fix errors in previous commands quickly.

History expansion takes place in two parts. The first is to determine which line from the history list should be used during substitution. The second is to select portions of that line for inclusion into the current one. The line selected from the history is called the *event*, and the portions of that line that are acted upon are called *words*. Various *modifiers* are available to manipulate the selected words. The line is broken into words in the same fashion that Bash does, so that several words surrounded by quotes are considered one word. History expansions are introduced by the appearance of the history expansion character, which is '!' by default. Only '\' and ''' may be used to escape the history expansion character.

Several shell options settable with the shopt builtin (see Section 4.2 [Bash Builtins], page 51) may be used to tailor the behavior of history expansion. If the histverify shell option is enabled, and Readline is being used, history substitutions are not immediately passed to the shell parser. Instead, the expanded line is reloaded into the Readline editing buffer for further modification. If Readline is being used, and the histreedit shell option is enabled, a failed history expansion will be reloaded into the Readline editing buffer for correction. The '-p' option to the history builtin command may be used to see what a history expansion will do before using it. The '-s' option to the history builtin may be used to add commands to the end of the history list without actually executing them, so that they are available for subsequent recall. This is most useful in conjunction with Readline.

The shell allows control of the various characters used by the history expansion mechanism with the histchars variable.

9.3.1 Event Designators

An event designator is a reference to a command line entry in the history list.

!   Start a history substitution, except when followed by a space, tab, the end of the line, '=' or '(' (when the extglob shell option is enabled using the shopt builtin).

!*n*   Refer to command line *n*.

!-*n*   Refer to the command *n* lines back.

!!   Refer to the previous command. This is a synonym for '!-1'.

!*string*   Refer to the most recent command starting with *string*.

!?*string*[?]

> Refer to the most recent command containing *string*. The trailing '?' may be omitted if the *string* is followed immediately by a newline.

^*string1*^*string2*^

> Quick Substitution. Repeat the last command, replacing *string1* with *string2*. Equivalent to !!:s/*string1*/*string2*/.

!#   The entire command line typed so far.

9.3.2 Word Designators

Word designators are used to select desired words from the event. A ':' separates the event specification from the word designator. It may be omitted if the word designator begins with a '^', '$', '*', '-', or '%'. Words are numbered from the beginning of the line, with the first word being denoted by 0 (zero). Words are inserted into the current line separated by single spaces.

For example,

!!   designates the preceding command. When you type this, the preceding command is repeated in toto.

!!:$ designates the last argument of the preceding command. This may be shortened to !$.

!fi:2   designates the second argument of the most recent command starting with the letters fi.

Here are the word designators:

0 (zero)   The 0th word. For many applications, this is the command word.

n   The *n*th word.

^   The first argument; that is, word 1.

$ The last argument.

%   The word matched by the most recent '?*string*?' search.

x-y   A range of words; '-*y*' abbreviates '0-*y*'.

*   All of the words, except the 0th. This is a synonym for '1-$'. It is not an error to use '*' if there is just one word in the event; the empty string is returned in that case.

*x**   Abbreviates '*x*-$'

x-   Abbreviates 'x-$' like 'x*', but omits the last word.

    If a word designator is supplied without an event specification, the previous command is used as the event.

9.3.3 Modifiers

    After the optional word designator, you can add a sequence of one or more of the following modifiers, each preceded by a ':'.

h   Remove a trailing pathname component, leaving only the head.

t   Remove all leading pathname components, leaving the tail.

r   Remove a trailing suffix of the form '.suffix', leaving the basename.

e   Remove all but the trailing suffix.

p   Print the new command but do not execute it.

q   Quote the substituted words, escaping further substitutions.

x   Quote the substituted words as with 'q', but break into words at spaces, tabs, and newlines.

s/old/new/
                    Substitute new for the first occurrence of old in the event line. Any delimiter may be used in place of '/'. The delimiter may be quoted in old and new with a single backslash. If '&' appears in new, it is replaced by old. A single backslash will quote the '&'. The final delimiter is optional if it is the last character on the input line.

&   Repeat the previous substitution.

g
a   Cause changes to be applied over the entire event line. Used in conjunction with 's', as in gs/old/new/, or with '&'.

G   Apply the following 's' modifier once to each word in the event.

10 Installing Bash

This chapter provides basic instructions for installing Bash on the various supported platforms. The distribution supports the GNU operating systems, nearly every version of Unix, and several non-Unix systems such as BeOS and Interix. Other independent ports exist for MS-DOS, OS/2, and Windows platforms.

10.1 Basic Installation

These are installation instructions for Bash.

The simplest way to compile Bash is:

1. cd to the directory containing the source code and type '`./configure`' to configure Bash for your system. If you're using csh on an old version of System V, you might need to type 'sh `./configure`' instead to prevent csh from trying to execute configure itself.

   Running `configure` takes some time. While running, it prints messages telling which features it is checking for.

2. Type '`make`' to compile Bash and build the bashbug bug reporting script.

3. Optionally, type '`make tests`' to run the Bash test suite.

4. Type '`make install`' to install bash and bashbug. This will also install the manual pages and Info file.

The `configure` shell script attempts to guess correct values for various system-dependent variables used during compilation. It uses those values to create a '`Makefile`' in each directory of the package (the top directory, the '`builtins`', '`doc`', and '`support`' directories, each directory under '`lib`', and several others). It also creates a '`config.h`' file containing system-dependent definitions. Finally, it creates a shell script named `config.status` that you can run in the future to recreate the current configuration, a file '`config.cache`' that saves the results of its tests to speed up reconfiguring, and a file '`config.log`' containing compiler output (useful mainly for debugging `configure`). If at some point '`config.cache`' contains results you don't want to keep, you may remove or edit it.

To find out more about the options and arguments that the `configure` script understands, type

```
bash-2.04$ ./configure --help
```

at the Bash prompt in your Bash source directory.

If you need to do unusual things to compile Bash, please try to figure out how `configure` could check whether or not to do them, and mail diffs or instructions to `bash-maintainers@gnu.org` so they can be considered for the next release.

The file 'configure.in' is used to create `configure` by a program called Autoconf. You only need 'configure.in' if you want to change it or regenerate `configure` using a newer version of Autoconf. If you do this, make sure you are using Autoconf version 2.50 or newer.

You can remove the program binaries and object files from the source code directory by typing 'make clean'. To also remove the files that `configure` created (so you can compile Bash for a different kind of computer), type 'make distclean'.

10.2 Compilers and Options

Some systems require unusual options for compilation or linking that the `configure` script does not know about. You can give `configure` initial values for variables by setting them in the environment. Using a Bourne-compatible shell, you can do that on the command line like this:

```
CC=c89 CFLAGS=-O2 LIBS=-lposix ./configure
```

On systems that have the env program, you can do it like this:

```
env CPPFLAGS=-I/usr/local/include LDFLAGS=-s ./configure
```

The configuration process uses GCC to build Bash if it is available.

10.3 Compiling For Multiple Architectures

You can compile Bash for more than one kind of computer at the same time, by placing the object files for each architecture in their own directory. To do this, you must use a version of make that supports the VPATH variable, such as GNU make. cd to the directory where you want the object files and executables to go and run the `configure` script from the source directory. You may need to supply the '--srcdir=PATH' argument to tell `configure` where the source files are. `configure` automatically checks for the source code in the directory that `configure` is in and in '..'.

If you have to use a make that does not supports the VPATH variable, you can compile Bash for one architecture at a time in the source code directory. After you have installed Bash for one architecture, use 'make distclean' before reconfiguring for another architecture.

Alternatively, if your system supports symbolic links, you can use the 'support/mkclone' script to create a build tree which has symbolic links

back to each file in the source directory. Here's an example that creates a build directory in the current directory from a source directory
'/usr/gnu/src/bash-2.0':

```
bash /usr/gnu/src/bash-2.0/support/mkclone
    -s /usr/gnu/src/bash-2.0 .
```

The mkclone script requires Bash, so you must have already built Bash
for at least one architecture before you can create build directories for
other architectures.

10.4 Installation Names

By default, 'make install' will install into '/usr/local/bin',
'/usr/local/man', etc. You can specify an installation prefix other than
'/usr/local' by giving configure the option '--prefix=*PATH*', or by
specifying a value for the DESTDIR 'make' variable when running 'make
install'.

You can specify separate installation prefixes for architecture-specific
files and architecture-independent files. If you give configure the option
'--exec-prefix=*PATH*', 'make install' will use *PATH* as the prefix for
installing programs and libraries. Documentation and other data files will
still use the regular prefix.

10.5 Specifying the System Type

There may be some features configure can not figure out automatically, but need to determine by the type of host Bash will run on. Usually
configure can figure that out, but if it prints a message saying it can not
guess the host type, give it the '--host=TYPE' option. 'TYPE' can either be
a short name for the system type, such as 'sun4', or a canonical name with
three fields: 'CPU-COMPANY-SYSTEM' (e.g., 'i386-unknown-freebsd4.2').

See the file 'support/config.sub' for the possible values of each field.

10.6 Sharing Defaults

If you want to set default values for configure scripts to
share, you can create a site shell script called config.site that
gives default values for variables like CC, cache_file, and prefix.
configure looks for 'PREFIX/share/config.site' if it exists, then
'PREFIX/etc/config.site' if it exists. Or, you can set the CONFIG_SITE
environment variable to the location of the site script. A warning: the
Bash configure looks for a site script, but not all configure scripts do.

10.7 Operation Controls

configure recognizes the following options to control how it operates.

--cache-file=*file*

>Use and save the results of the tests in *file* instead of '`./config.cache`'. Set *file* to '/dev/null' to disable caching, for debugging configure.

--help   Print a summary of the options to configure, and exit.

--quiet
--silent
-q   Do not print messages saying which checks are being made.

--srcdir=*dir*

>Look for the Bash source code in directory *dir*. Usually configure can determine that directory automatically.

--version Print the version of Autoconf used to generate the configure script, and exit.

configure also accepts some other, not widely used, boilerplate options. '`configure --help`' prints the complete list.

10.8 Optional Features

The Bash configure has a number of '--enable-*feature*' options, where *feature* indicates an optional part of Bash. There are also several '--with-*package*' options, where *package* is something like 'bash-malloc' or 'purify'. To turn off the default use of a package, use '--without-*package*'. To configure Bash without a feature that is enabled by default, use '--disable-*feature*'.

Here is a complete list of the '--enable-' and '--with-' options that the Bash configure recognizes.

--with-afs

>Define if you are using the Andrew File System from Transarc.

--with-bash-malloc

>Use the Bash version of malloc in the directory '1ib/malloc'. This is not the same malloc that appears in GNU libc, but an older version originally derived from the 4.2 BSD malloc. This malloc is very fast, but wastes some space on each allocation. This option is enabled by default. The 'NOTES' file contains a list of systems for which this

should be turned off, and `configure` disables this option automatically for a number of systems.

`--with-curses`

Use the curses library instead of the termcap library. This should be supplied if your system has an inadequate or incomplete termcap database.

`--with-gnu-malloc`

A synonym for `--with-bash-malloc`.

`--with-installed-readline[=PREFIX]`

Define this to make Bash link with a locally-installed version of Readline rather than the version in 'lib/readline'. This works only with Readline 5.0 and later versions. If *PRE-FIX* is yes or not supplied, `configure` uses the values of the make variables `includedir` and `libdir`, which are subdirectories of `prefix` by default, to find the installed version of Readline if it is not in the standard system include and library directories. If *PREFIX* is no, Bash links with the version in 'lib/readline'. If *PREFIX* is set to any other value, `configure` treats it as a directory pathname and looks for the installed version of Readline in subdirectories of that directory (include files in *PREFIX*/include and the library in *PREFIX*/lib).

`--with-purify`

Define this to use the Purify memory allocation checker from Rational Software.

`--enable-minimal-config`

This produces a shell with minimal features, close to the historical Bourne shell.

There are several '`--enable-`' options that alter how Bash is compiled and linked, rather than changing run-time features.

`--enable-largefile`

Enable support for large files[1] if the operating system requires special compiler options to build programs which can access large files. This is enabled by default, if the operating system provides large file support.

`--enable-profiling`

This builds a Bash binary that produces profiling information to be processed by `gprof` each time it is executed.

---

[1] `http://opengroup.org/platform/lfs.html`

`--enable-static-link`
> This causes Bash to be linked statically, if gcc is being used.
> This could be used to build a version to use as root's shell.

The 'minimal-config' option can be used to disable all of the following options, but it is processed first, so individual options may be enabled using 'enable-*feature*'.

All of the following options except for 'disabled-builtins' and 'xpg-echo-default' are enabled by default, unless the operating system does not provide the necessary support.

`--enable-alias`
> Allow alias expansion and include the alias and unalias builtins (see Section 6.6 [Aliases], page 95).

`--enable-arith-for-command`
> Include support for the alternate form of the for command that behaves like the C language for statement (see Section 3.2.4.1 [Looping Constructs], page 13).

`--enable-array-variables`
> Include support for one-dimensional array shell variables (see Section 6.7 [Arrays], page 96).

`--enable-bang-history`
> Include support for csh-like history substitution (see Section 9.3 [History Interaction], page 147).

`--enable-brace-expansion`
> Include csh-like brace expansion (b{a,b}c $\mapsto$ bac bbc). See Section 3.5.1 [Brace Expansion], page 23, for a complete description.

`--enable-command-timing`
> Include support for recognizing time as a reserved word and for displaying timing statistics for the pipeline following time (see Section 3.2.2 [Pipelines], page 11). This allows pipelines as well as shell builtins and functions to be timed.

`--enable-cond-command`
> Include support for the [[conditional command. (see Section 3.2.4.2 [Conditional Constructs], page 14).

`--enable-cond-regexp`
> Include support for matching POSIX regular expressions using the '=~' binary operator in the [[conditional command. (see Section 3.2.4.2 [Conditional Constructs], page 14).

`--enable-debugger`

> Include support for the bash debugger (distributed separately).

`--enable-directory-stack`

> Include support for a csh-like directory stack and the pushd, popd, and dirs builtins (see Section 6.8 [The Directory Stack], page 98).

`--enable-disabled-builtins`

> Allow builtin commands to be invoked via 'builtin xxx' even after xxx has been disabled using 'enable -n xxx'. See Section 4.2 [Bash Builtins], page 51, for details of the builtin and enable builtin commands.

`--enable-dparen-arithmetic`

> Include support for the ((...)) command (see Section 3.2.4.2 [Conditional Constructs], page 14).

`--enable-extended-glob`

> Include support for the extended pattern matching features described above under Section 3.5.8.1 [Pattern Matching], page 31.

`--enable-help-builtin`

> Include the help builtin, which displays help on shell builtins and variables (see Section 4.2 [Bash Builtins], page 51).

`--enable-history`

> Include command history and the fc and history builtin commands (see Section 9.1 [Bash History Facilities], page 145).

`--enable-job-control`

> This enables the job control features (see Chapter 7 [Job Control], page 107), if the operating system supports them.

`--enable-multibyte`

> This enables support for multibyte characters if the operating system provides the necessary support.

`--enable-net-redirections`

> This enables the special handling of filenames of the form /dev/tcp/*host*/*port* and /dev/udp/*host*/*port* when used in redirections (see Section 3.6 [Redirections], page 32).

`--enable-process-substitution`

> This enables process substitution (see Section 3.5.6 [Process Substitution], page 29) if the operating system provides the necessary support.

`--enable-progcomp`

Enable the programmable completion facilities (see Section 8.6 [Programmable Completion], page 138). If Readline is not enabled, this option has no effect.

`--enable-prompt-string-decoding`

Turn on the interpretation of a number of backslash-escaped characters in the $PS1, $PS2, $PS3, and $PS4 prompt strings. See Section 6.9 [Printing a Prompt], page 99, for a complete list of prompt string escape sequences.

`--enable-readline`

Include support for command-line editing and history with the Bash version of the Readline library (see Chapter 8 [Command Line Editing], page 113).

`--enable-restricted`

Include support for a *restricted shell*. If this is enabled, Bash, when called as rbash, enters a restricted mode. See Section 6.10 [The Restricted Shell], page 101, for a description of restricted mode.

`--enable-select`

Include the select builtin, which allows the generation of simple menus (see Section 3.2.4.2 [Conditional Constructs], page 14).

`--enable-separate-helpfiles`

Use external files for the documentation displayed by the help builtin instead of storing the text internally.

`--enable-single-help-strings`

Store the text displayed by the help builtin as a single string for each help topic. This aids in translating the text to different languages. You may need to disable this if your compiler cannot handle very long string literals.

`--enable-strict-posix-default`

Make Bash POSIX-conformant by default (see Section 6.11 [Bash POSIX Mode], page 102).

`--enable-usg-echo-default`

A synonym for --enable-xpg-echo-default.

`--enable-xpg-echo-default`

Make the echo builtin expand backslash-escaped characters by default, without requiring the '-e' option. This sets the default value of the xpg_echo shell option to on, which makes

the Bash echo behave more like the version specified in the
Single Unix Specification, version 3. See Section 4.2 [Bash
Builtins], page 51, for a description of the escape sequences
that echo recognizes.

The file 'config-top.h' contains C Preprocessor '#define' statements
for options which are not settable from configure. Some of these are not
meant to be changed; beware of the consequences if you do. Read the
comments associated with each definition for more information about its
effect.

Appendix A Reporting Bugs

Please report all bugs you find in Bash. But first, you should make sure that it really is a bug, and that it appears in the latest version of Bash. The latest version of Bash is always available for FTP from ftp://ftp.gnu.org/pub/bash/.

Once you have determined that a bug actually exists, use the bashbug command to submit a bug report. If you have a fix, you are encouraged to mail that as well! Suggestions and 'philosophical' bug reports may be mailed to bug-bash@gnu.org or posted to the Usenet newsgroup gnu.bash.bug.

All bug reports should include:

- The version number of Bash.
- The hardware and operating system.
- The compiler used to compile Bash.
- A description of the bug behaviour.
- A short script or 'recipe' which exercises the bug and may be used to reproduce it.

bashbug inserts the first three items automatically into the template it provides for filing a bug report.

Please send all reports concerning this manual to the publisher at info@network-theory.co.uk. These will be evaluated and forwarded to the GNU Bash maintainer chet@po.CWRU.Edu as appropriate.

Appendix B   Major Differences From The Bourne Shell

Bash implements essentially the same grammar, parameter and variable expansion, redirection, and quoting as the Bourne Shell. Bash uses the POSIX standard as the specification of how these features are to be implemented. There are some differences between the traditional Bourne shell and Bash; this section quickly details the differences of significance. A number of these differences are explained in greater depth in previous sections. This section uses the version of sh included in SVR4.2 (the last version of the historical Bourne shell) as the baseline reference.

- Bash is POSIX-conformant, even where the POSIX specification differs from traditional sh behavior (see Section 6.11 [Bash POSIX Mode], page 102).

- Bash has multi-character invocation options (see Section 6.1 [Invoking Bash], page 85).

- Bash has command-line editing (see Chapter 8 [Command Line Editing], page 113) and the bind builtin.

- Bash provides a programmable word completion mechanism (see Section 8.6 [Programmable Completion], page 138), and two builtin commands, complete and compgen, to manipulate it.

- Bash has command history (see Section 9.1 [Bash History Facilities], page 145) and the history and fc builtins to manipulate it. The Bash history list maintains timestamp information and uses the value of the HISTTIMEFORMAT variable to display it.

- Bash implements csh-like history expansion (see Section 9.3 [History Interaction], page 147).

- Bash has one-dimensional array variables (see Section 6.7 [Arrays], page 96), and the appropriate variable expansions and assignment syntax to use them. Several of the Bash builtins take options to act on arrays. Bash provides a number of built-in array variables.

- The $'...' quoting syntax, which expands ANSI-C backslash-escaped characters in the text between the single quotes, is supported (see Section 3.1.2.4 [ANSI-C Quoting], page 9).

- Bash supports the $"..." quoting syntax to do locale-specific translation of the characters between the double quotes. The '-D', '--dump-strings', and '--dump-po-strings' invocation options list the translatable strings found in a script (see Section 3.1.2.5 [Locale Translation], page 10).

- Bash implements the ! keyword to negate the return value of a pipeline (see Section 3.2.2 [Pipelines], page 11). Very useful when an if statement needs to act only if a test fails. The Bash '-o pipefail' option to set will cause a pipeline to return a failure status if any command fails.

- Bash has the time reserved word and command timing (see Section 3.2.2 [Pipelines], page 11). The display of the timing statistics may be controlled with the TIMEFORMAT variable.

- Bash implements the for ((expr1 ; expr2 ; expr3)) arithmetic for command, similar to the C language (see Section 3.2.4.1 [Looping Constructs], page 13).

- Bash includes the select compound command, which allows the generation of simple menus (see Section 3.2.4.2 [Conditional Constructs], page 14).

- Bash includes the [[compound command, which makes conditional testing part of the shell grammar (see Section 3.2.4.2 [Conditional Constructs], page 14), including optional regular expression matching.

- Bash provides optional case-insensitive matching for the case and [[constructs.

- Bash includes brace expansion (see Section 3.5.1 [Brace Expansion], page 23) and tilde expansion (see Section 3.5.2 [Tilde Expansion], page 24).

- Bash implements command aliases and the alias and unalias builtins (see Section 6.6 [Aliases], page 95).

- Bash provides shell arithmetic, the ((compound command (see Section 3.2.4.2 [Conditional Constructs], page 14), and arithmetic expansion (see Section 6.5 [Shell Arithmetic], page 94).

- Variables present in the shell's initial environment are automatically exported to child processes. The Bourne shell does not normally do this unless the variables are explicitly marked using the export command.

- Bash supports the '+=' assignment operator, which appends to the value of the variable named on the left hand side.

- Bash includes the POSIX pattern removal '%', '#', '%%' and '##' expansions to remove leading or trailing substrings from variable values (see Section 3.5.3 [Shell Parameter Expansion], page 25).

- The expansion ${#xx}, which returns the length of ${xx}, is supported (see Section 3.5.3 [Shell Parameter Expansion], page 25).

- The expansion ${var:offset[:length]}, which expands to the substring of var's value of length *length*, beginning at *offset*, is present (see Section 3.5.3 [Shell Parameter Expansion], page 25).

- The expansion ${var/[/]pattern[/replacement]}, which matches *pattern* and replaces it with *replacement* in the value of var, is available (see Section 3.5.3 [Shell Parameter Expansion], page 25).

- The expansion ${!prefix*}, which expands to the names of all shell variables whose names begin with *prefix*, is available (see Section 3.5.3 [Shell Parameter Expansion], page 25).

- Bash has *indirect* variable expansion using ${!word} (see Section 3.5.3 [Shell Parameter Expansion], page 25).

- Bash can expand positional parameters beyond $9 using ${num}.

- The POSIX $() form of command substitution is implemented (see Section 3.5.4 [Command Substitution], page 28), and preferred to the Bourne shell's ' ' (which is also implemented for backwards compatibility).

- Bash has process substitution (see Section 3.5.6 [Process Substitution], page 29).

- Bash automatically assigns variables that provide information about the current user (UID, EUID, and GROUPS), the current host (HOSTTYPE, OSTYPE, MACHTYPE, and HOSTNAME), and the instance of Bash that is running (BASH, BASH_VERSION, and BASH_VERSINFO). See Section 5.2 [Bash Variables], page 74, for details.

- The IFS variable is used to split only the results of expansion, not all words (see Section 3.5.7 [Word Splitting], page 29). This closes a longstanding shell security hole.

- Bash implements the full set of POSIX filename expansion operators, including *character classes*, *equivalence classes*, and *collating symbols* (see Section 3.5.8 [Filename Expansion], page 30).

- Bash implements extended pattern matching features when the extglob shell option is enabled (see Section 3.5.8.1 [Pattern Matching], page 31).

- It is possible to have a variable and a function with the same name; sh does not separate the two name spaces.

- Bash functions are permitted to have local variables using the local builtin, and thus useful recursive functions may be written (see Section 4.2 [Bash Builtins], page 51).

- Variable assignments preceding commands affect only that command, even builtins and functions (see Section 3.7.4 [Environment], page 39). In sh, all variable assignments preceding commands are global unless the command is executed from the file system.

- Bash performs filename expansion on filenames specified as operands to input and output redirection operators (see Section 3.6 [Redirections], page 32).
- Bash contains the '<>' redirection operator, allowing a file to be opened for both reading and writing, and the '&>' redirection operator, for directing standard output and standard error to the same file (see Section 3.6 [Redirections], page 32).
- Bash includes the '<<<' redirection operator, allowing a string to be used as the standard input to a command.
- Bash implements the '[n]<&word' and '[n]>&word' redirection operators, which move one file descriptor to another.
- Bash treats a number of filenames specially when they are used in redirection operators (see Section 3.6 [Redirections], page 32).
- Bash can open network connections to arbitrary machines and services with the redirection operators (see Section 3.6 [Redirections], page 32).
- The noclobber option is available to avoid overwriting existing files with output redirection (see Section 4.3 [The Set Builtin], page 66). The '>|' redirection operator may be used to override noclobber.
- The Bash cd and pwd builtins (see Section 4.1 [Bourne Shell Builtins], page 43) each take '-L' and '-P' options to switch between logical and physical modes.
- Bash allows a function to override a builtin with the same name, and provides access to that builtin's functionality within the function via the builtin and command builtins (see Section 4.2 [Bash Builtins], page 51).
- The command builtin allows selective disabling of functions when command lookup is performed (see Section 4.2 [Bash Builtins], page 51).
- Individual builtins may be enabled or disabled using the enable builtin (see Section 4.2 [Bash Builtins], page 51).
- The Bash exec builtin takes additional options that allow users to control the contents of the environment passed to the executed command, and what the zeroth argument to the command is to be (see Section 4.1 [Bourne Shell Builtins], page 43).
- Shell functions may be exported to children via the environment using export -f (see Section 3.3 [Shell Functions], page 18).
- The Bash export, readonly, and declare builtins can take a '-f' option to act on shell functions, a '-p' option to display variables with various attributes set in a format that can be used as shell input, a '-n' option to remove various variable attributes, and 'name=value' arguments to set variable attributes and values simultaneously.

- The Bash hash builtin allows a name to be associated with an arbitrary filename, even when that filename cannot be found by searching the $PATH, using 'hash -p' (see Section 4.1 [Bourne Shell Builtins], page 43).

- Bash includes a help builtin for quick reference to shell facilities (see Section 4.2 [Bash Builtins], page 51).

- The printf builtin is available to display formatted output (see Section 4.2 [Bash Builtins], page 51).

- The Bash read builtin (see Section 4.2 [Bash Builtins], page 51) will read a line ending in '\' with the '-r' option, and will use the REPLY variable as a default if no non-option arguments are supplied. The Bash read builtin also accepts a prompt string with the '-p' option and will use Readline to obtain the line when given the '-e' option. The read builtin also has additional options to control input: the '-s' option will turn off echoing of input characters as they are read, the '-t' option will allow read to time out if input does not arrive within a specified number of seconds, the '-n' option will allow reading only a specified number of characters rather than a full line, and the '-d' option will read until a particular character rather than newline.

- The return builtin may be used to abort execution of scripts executed with the . or source builtins (see Section 4.1 [Bourne Shell Builtins], page 43).

- Bash includes the shopt builtin, for finer control of shell optional capabilities (see Section 4.2 [Bash Builtins], page 51), and allows these options to be set and unset at shell invocation (see Section 6.1 [Invoking Bash], page 85).

- Bash has much more optional behavior controllable with the set builtin (see Section 4.3 [The Set Builtin], page 66).

- The '-x' (xtrace) option displays commands other than simple commands when performing an execution trace (see Section 4.3 [The Set Builtin], page 66).

- The test builtin (see Section 4.1 [Bourne Shell Builtins], page 43) is slightly different, as it implements the POSIX algorithm, which specifies the behavior based on the number of arguments.

- Bash includes the caller builtin, which displays the context of any active subroutine call (a shell function or a script executed with the . or source builtins). This supports the bash debugger.

- The trap builtin (see Section 4.1 [Bourne Shell Builtins], page 43) allows a DEBUG pseudo-signal specification, similar to EXIT. Commands specified with a DEBUG trap are executed before every simple command, for command, case command, select command, every arithmetic for command, and before the first command executes in a shell function. The DEBUG trap is not inherited by shell functions unless the function has been given the trace attribute or the functrace option has been enabled using the shopt builtin. The extdebug shell option has additional effects on the DEBUG trap.

The trap builtin (see Section 4.1 [Bourne Shell Builtins], page 43) allows an ERR pseudo-signal specification, similar to EXIT and DEBUG. Commands specified with an ERR trap are executed after a simple command fails, with a few exceptions. The ERR trap is not inherited by shell functions unless the -o errtrace option to the set builtin is enabled.

The trap builtin (see Section 4.1 [Bourne Shell Builtins], page 43) allows a RETURN pseudo-signal specification, similar to EXIT and DEBUG. Commands specified with an RETURN trap are executed before execution resumes after a shell function or a shell script executed with . or source returns. The RETURN trap is not inherited by shell functions unless the function has been given the trace attribute or the functrace option has been enabled using the shopt builtin.

- The Bash type builtin is more extensive and gives more information about the names it finds (see Section 4.2 [Bash Builtins], page 51).

- The Bash umask builtin permits a '-p' option to cause the output to be displayed in the form of a umask command that may be reused as input (see Section 4.1 [Bourne Shell Builtins], page 43).

- Bash implements a csh-like directory stack, and provides the pushd, popd, and dirs builtins to manipulate it (see Section 6.8 [The Directory Stack], page 98). Bash also makes the directory stack visible as the value of the DIRSTACK shell variable.

- Bash interprets special backslash-escaped characters in the prompt strings when interactive (see Section 6.9 [Printing a Prompt], page 99).

- The Bash restricted mode is more useful (see Section 6.10 [The Restricted Shell], page 101); the SVR4.2 shell restricted mode is too limited.

- The disown builtin can remove a job from the internal shell job table (see Section 7.2 [Job Control Builtins], page 108) or suppress the sending of SIGHUP to a job when the shell exits as the result of a SIGHUP.

- Bash includes a number of features to support a separate debugger for shell scripts.

- The SVR4.2 shell has two privilege-related builtins (mldmode and priv) not present in Bash.

- Bash does not have the stop or newgrp builtins.
- Bash does not use the SHACCT variable or perform shell accounting.
- The SVR4.2 sh uses a TIMEOUT variable like Bash uses TMOUT.

More features unique to Bash may be found in Chapter 6 [Bash Features], page 85.

B.1 Implementation Differences From The SVR4.2 Shell

Since Bash is a completely new implementation, it does not suffer from many of the limitations of the SVR4.2 shell. For instance:

- Bash does not fork a subshell when redirecting into or out of a shell control structure such as an if or while statement.
- Bash does not allow unbalanced quotes. The SVR4.2 shell will silently insert a needed closing quote at EOF under certain circumstances. This can be the cause of some hard-to-find errors.
- The SVR4.2 shell uses a baroque memory management scheme based on trapping SIGSEGV. If the shell is started from a process with SIGSEGV blocked (e.g., by using the system() C library function call), it misbehaves badly.
- In a questionable attempt at security, the SVR4.2 shell, when invoked without the '-p' option, will alter its real and effective UID and GID if they are less than some magic threshold value, commonly 100. This can lead to unexpected results.
- The SVR4.2 shell does not allow users to trap SIGSEGV, SIGALRM, or SIGCHLD.
- The SVR4.2 shell does not allow the IFS, MAILCHECK, PATH, PS1, or PS2 variables to be unset.
- The SVR4.2 shell treats '^' as the undocumented equivalent of '|'.
- Bash allows multiple option arguments when it is invoked (-x -v); the SVR4.2 shell allows only one option argument (-xv). In fact, some versions of the shell dump core if the second argument begins with a '-'.
- The SVR4.2 shell exits a script if any builtin fails; Bash exits a script only if one of the POSIX special builtins fails, and only for certain failures, as enumerated in the POSIX standard.
- The SVR4.2 shell behaves differently when invoked as jsh (it turns on job control).

Appendix C Copying This Manual

Version 1.2, November 2002

Copyright © 2000,2001,2002 Free Software Foundation, Inc.

51 Franklin St, Fifth Floor, Boston, MA 02110-1301, USA

0. PREAMBLE

The purpose of this License is to make a manual, textbook, or other functional and useful document *free* in the sense of freedom: to assure everyone the effective freedom to copy and redistribute it, with or without modifying it, either commercially or noncommercially. Secondarily, this License preserves for the author and publisher a way to get credit for their work, while not being considered responsible for modifications made by others.

This License is a kind of "copyleft", which means that derivative works of the document must themselves be free in the same sense. It complements the GNU General Public License, which is a copyleft license designed for free software.

We have designed this License in order to use it for manuals for free software, because free software needs free documentation: a free program should come with manuals providing the same freedoms that the software does. But this License is not limited to software manuals; it can be used for any textual work, regardless of subject matter or whether it is published as a printed book. We recommend this License principally for works whose purpose is instruction or reference.

1. APPLICABILITY AND DEFINITIONS

This License applies to any manual or other work, in any medium, that contains a notice placed by the copyright holder saying it can be distributed under the terms of this License. Such a notice grants a worldwide, royalty-free license, unlimited in duration, to use that work under the conditions stated herein. The "Document", below, refers to any such manual or work. Any member of the public is a licensee, and is addressed as "you". You accept the license if you copy, modify or distribute the work in a way requiring permission under copyright law.

A "Modified Version" of the Document means any work containing the Document or a portion of it, either copied verbatim, or with modifications and/or translated into another language.

A "Secondary Section" is a named appendix or a front-matter section of the Document that deals exclusively with the relationship of the publishers or authors of the Document to the Document's overall subject (or to related matters) and contains nothing that could fall directly within that overall subject. (Thus, if the Document is in part a textbook of mathematics, a

Secondary Section may not explain any mathematics.) The relationship could be a matter of historical connection with the subject or with related matters, or of legal, commercial, philosophical, ethical or political position regarding them.

The "Invariant Sections" are certain Secondary Sections whose titles are designated, as being those of Invariant Sections, in the notice that says that the Document is released under this License. If a section does not fit the above definition of Secondary then it is not allowed to be designated as Invariant. The Document may contain zero Invariant Sections. If the Document does not identify any Invariant Sections then there are none.

The "Cover Texts" are certain short passages of text that are listed, as Front-Cover Texts or Back-Cover Texts, in the notice that says that the Document is released under this License. A Front-Cover Text may be at most 5 words, and a Back-Cover Text may be at most 25 words.

A "Transparent" copy of the Document means a machine-readable copy, represented in a format whose specification is available to the general public, that is suitable for revising the document straightforwardly with generic text editors or (for images composed of pixels) generic paint pro-grams or (for drawings) some widely available drawing editor, and that is suitable for input to text formatters or for automatic translation to a variety of formats suitable for input to text formatters. A copy made in an otherwise Transparent file format whose markup, or absence of markup, has been arranged to thwart or discourage subsequent modification by readers is not Transparent. An image format is not Transparent if used for any substantial amount of text. A copy that is not "Transparent" is called "Opaque".

Examples of suitable formats for Transparent copies include plain ASCII without markup, Texinfo input format, LaTeX input format, SGML or XML using a publicly available DTD, and standard-conforming simple HTML, PostScript or PDF designed for human modification. Examples of trans-parent image formats include PNG, XCF and JPG. Opaque formats include proprietary formats that can be read and edited only by proprietary word processors, SGML or XML for which the DTD and/or processing tools are not generally available, and the machine-generated HTML, PostScript or PDF produced by some word processors for output purposes only.

The "Title Page" means, for a printed book, the title page itself, plus such following pages as are needed to hold, legibly, the material this License requires to appear in the title page. For works in formats which do not have any title page as such, "Title Page" means the text near the most prominent appearance of the work's title, preceding the beginning of the body of the text.

A section "Entitled XYZ" means a named subunit of the Document whose title either is precisely XYZ or contains XYZ in parentheses following text that translates XYZ in another language. (Here XYZ stands for a specific section name mentioned below, such as "Acknowledgements", "Dedications", "Endorsements", or "History".) To "Preserve the Title" of such a section when you modify the Document means that it remains a section "Entitled XYZ" according to this definition.

The Document may include Warranty Disclaimers next to the notice which states that this License applies to the Document. These Warranty Disclaimers are considered to be included by reference in this License, but only as regards disclaiming warranties: any other implication that these Warranty Disclaimers may have is void and has no effect on the meaning of this License.

2. VERBATIM COPYING

You may copy and distribute the Document in any medium, either commercially or noncommercially, provided that this License, the copyright notices, and the license notice saying this License applies to the Document are reproduced in all copies, and that you add no other conditions whatsoever to those of this License. You may not use technical measures to obstruct or control the reading or further copying of the copies you make or distribute. However, you may accept compensation in exchange for copies. If you distribute a large enough number of copies you must also follow the conditions in section 3.

You may also lend copies, under the same conditions stated above, and you may publicly display copies.

3. COPYING IN QUANTITY

If you publish printed copies (or copies in media that commonly have printed covers) of the Document, numbering more than 100, and the Document's license notice requires Cover Texts, you must enclose the copies in covers that carry, clearly and legibly, all these Cover Texts: Front-Cover Texts on the front cover, and Back-Cover Texts on the back cover. Both covers must also clearly and legibly identify you as the publisher of these copies. The front cover must present the full title with all words of the title equally prominent and visible. You may add other material on the covers in addition. Copying with changes limited to the covers, as long as they preserve the title of the Document and satisfy these conditions, can be treated as verbatim copying in other respects.

If the required texts for either cover are too voluminous to fit legibly, you should put the first ones listed (as many as fit reasonably) on the actual cover, and continue the rest onto adjacent pages.

If you publish or distribute Opaque copies of the Document numbering more than 100, you must either include a machine-readable Transparent copy along with each Opaque copy, or state in or with each Opaque copy a computer-network location from which the general network-using public has access to download using public-standard network protocols a complete Transparent copy of the Document, free of added material. If you use the latter option, you must take reasonably prudent steps, when you begin distribution of Opaque copies in quantity, to ensure that this Transparent copy will remain thus accessible at the stated location until at least one year after the last time you distribute an Opaque copy (directly or through your agents or retailers) of that edition to the public.

It is requested, but not required, that you contact the authors of the Document well before redistributing any large number of copies, to give them a chance to provide you with an updated version of the Document.

4. MODIFICATIONS

You may copy and distribute a Modified Version of the Document under the conditions of sections 2 and 3 above, provided that you release the Modified Version under precisely this License, with the Modified Version filling the role of the Document, thus licensing distribution and modification of the Modified Version to whoever possesses a copy of it. In addition, you must do these things in the Modified Version:

A. Use in the Title Page (and on the covers, if any) a title distinct from that of the Document, and from those of previous versions (which should, if there were any, be listed in the History section of the Document). You may use the same title as a previous version if the original publisher of that version gives permission.

B. List on the Title Page, as authors, one or more persons or entities responsible for authorship of the modifications in the Modified Version, together with at least five of the principal authors of the Document (all of its principal authors, if it has fewer than five), unless they release you from this requirement.

C. State on the Title page the name of the publisher of the Modified Version, as the publisher.

D. Preserve all the copyright notices of the Document.

E. Add an appropriate copyright notice for your modifications adjacent to the other copyright notices.

F. Include, immediately after the copyright notices, a license notice giving the public permission to use the Modified Version under the terms of this License, in the form shown in the Addendum below.

G. Preserve in that license notice the full lists of Invariant Sections and required Cover Texts given in the Document's license notice.

H. Include an unaltered copy of this License.

I. Preserve the section Entitled "History", Preserve its Title, and add to it an item stating at least the title, year, new authors, and publisher of the Modified Version as given on the Title Page. If there is no section Entitled "History" in the Document, create one stating the title, year, authors, and publisher of the Document as given on its Title Page, then add an item describing the Modified Version as stated in the previous sentence.

J. Preserve the network location, if any, given in the Document for public access to a Transparent copy of the Document, and likewise the network locations given in the Document for previous versions it was based on. These may be placed in the "History" section. You may omit a network location for a work that was published at least four years before the Document itself, or if the original publisher of the version it refers to gives permission.

K. For any section Entitled "Acknowledgements" or "Dedications", Preserve the Title of the section, and preserve in the section all the substance and tone of each of the contributor acknowledgements and/or dedications given therein.

L. Preserve all the Invariant Sections of the Document, unaltered in their text and in their titles. Section numbers or the equivalent are not considered part of the section titles.

M. Delete any section Entitled "Endorsements". Such a section may not be included in the Modified Version.

N. Do not retitle any existing section to be Entitled "Endorsements" or to conflict in title with any Invariant Section.

O. Preserve any Warranty Disclaimers.

If the Modified Version includes new front-matter sections or appendices that qualify as Secondary Sections and contain no material copied from the Document, you may at your option designate some or all of these sections as invariant. To do this, add their titles to the list of Invariant Sections in the Modified Version's license notice. These titles must be distinct from any other section titles.

You may add a section Entitled "Endorsements", provided it contains nothing but endorsements of your Modified Version by various parties— for example, statements of peer review or that the text has been approved by an organization as the authoritative definition of a standard.

You may add a passage of up to five words as a Front-Cover Text, and a passage of up to 25 words as a Back-Cover Text, to the end of the list of Cover Texts in the Modified Version. Only one passage of Front-Cover Text and one of Back-Cover Text may be added by (or through arrangements made by) any one entity. If the Document already includes a cover text for the same cover, previously added by you or by arrangement made by the same entity you are acting on behalf of, you may not add another; but you may replace the old one, on explicit permission from the previous publisher that added the old one.

The author(s) and publisher(s) of the Document do not by this License give permission to use their names for publicity for or to assert or imply endorsement of any Modified Version.

5. COMBINING DOCUMENTS

You may combine the Document with other documents released under this License, under the terms defined in section 4 above for modified versions, provided that you include in the combination all of the Invariant Sections of all of the original documents, unmodified, and list them all as Invariant Sections of your combined work in its license notice, and that you preserve all their Warranty Disclaimers.

The combined work need only contain one copy of this License, and multiple identical Invariant Sections may be replaced with a single copy. If there are multiple Invariant Sections with the same name but different contents, make the title of each such section unique by adding at the end of it, in parentheses, the name of the original author or publisher of that section if known, or else a unique number. Make the same adjustment to the section titles in the list of Invariant Sections in the license notice of the combined work.

In the combination, you must combine any sections Entitled "History" in the various original documents, forming one section Entitled "History"; likewise combine any sections Entitled "Acknowledgements", and any sections Entitled "Dedications". You must delete all sections Entitled "Endorsements."

6. COLLECTIONS OF DOCUMENTS

You may make a collection consisting of the Document and other documents released under this License, and replace the individual copies of this License in the various documents with a single copy that is included in the collection, provided that you follow the rules of this License for verbatim copying of each of the documents in all other respects.

You may extract a single document from such a collection, and distribute it individually under this License, provided you insert a copy of this License into the extracted document, and follow this License in all other respects regarding verbatim copying of that document.

7. AGGREGATION WITH INDEPENDENT WORKS

A compilation of the Document or its derivatives with other separate and independent documents or works, in or on a volume of a storage or distribution medium, is called an "aggregate" if the copyright resulting from the compilation is not used to limit the legal rights of the compilation's users beyond what the individual works permit. When the Document is included in an aggregate, this License does not apply to the other works in the aggregate which are not themselves derivative works of the Document.

If the Cover Text requirement of section 3 is applicable to these copies of the Document, then if the Document is less than one half of the entire aggregate, the Document's Cover Texts may be placed on covers that bracket the Document within the aggregate, or the electronic equivalent of covers if the Document is in electronic form. Otherwise they must appear on printed covers that bracket the whole aggregate.

8. TRANSLATION

Translation is considered a kind of modification, so you may distribute translations of the Document under the terms of section 4. Replacing Invariant Sections with translations requires special permission from their copyright holders, but you may include translations of some or all Invariant Sections in addition to the original versions of these Invariant Sections. You may include a translation of this License, and all the license notices in the Document, and any Warranty Disclaimers, provided that you also include the original English version of this License and the original versions of those notices and disclaimers. In case of a disagreement between the translation and the original version of this License or a notice or disclaimer, the original version will prevail.

If a section in the Document is Entitled "Acknowledgements", "Dedications", or "History", the requirement (section 4) to Preserve its Title (section 1) will typically require changing the actual title.

9. TERMINATION

You may not copy, modify, sublicense, or distribute the Document except as expressly provided for under this License. Any other attempt to copy, modify, sublicense or distribute the Document is void, and will automatically terminate your rights under this License. However, parties who have received copies, or rights, from you under this License will not have their licenses terminated so long as such parties remain in full compliance.

10. FUTURE REVISIONS OF THIS LICENSE

The Free Software Foundation may publish new, revised versions of the GNU Free Documentation License from time to time. Such new versions will be similar in spirit to the present version, but may differ in detail to address new problems or concerns. See http://www.gnu.org/copyleft/.

Each version of the License is given a distinguishing version number. If the Document specifies that a particular numbered version of this License "or any later version" applies to it, you have the option of following the terms and conditions either of that specified version or of any later version that has been published (not as a draft) by the Free Software Foundation. If the Document does not specify a version number of this License, you may choose any version ever published (not as a draft) by the Free Software Foundation.

ADDENDUM: How to use this License for your documents

To use this License in a document you have written, include a copy of the License in the document and put the following copyright and license notices just after the title page:

> Copyright (C) *year your name*.
> Permission is granted to copy, distribute and/or modify
> this document under the terms of the GNU Free
> Documentation License, Version 1.2 or any later version
> published by the Free Software Foundation; with no
> Invariant Sections, no Front-Cover Texts, and no
> Back-Cover Texts. A copy of the license is included in
> the section entitled ''GNU Free Documentation License''.

If you have Invariant Sections, Front-Cover Texts and Back-Cover Texts, replace the "with...Texts." line with this:

> with the Invariant Sections being *list their*
> *titles*, with the Front-Cover Texts being *list*, and
> with the Back-Cover Texts being *list*.

If you have Invariant Sections without Cover Texts, or some other combination of the three, merge those two alternatives to suit the situation.

If your document contains nontrivial examples of program code, we recommend releasing these examples in parallel under your choice of free software license, such as the GNU General Public License, to permit their use in free software.

History

This section gives the history of the modifications made to the manual by the publisher, as required by the GNU Free Documentation License.

9/2005 "Bash Reference Manual" (original 3.2 release)
> Chet Ramey and Brian Fox
> Publisher: Free Software Foundation.

10/2006 "GNU Bash Reference Manual"
> Edited for publication by Brian Gough
> Publisher: Network Theory Ltd.
> Changed title, as given above. Added publisher's preface. Minor changes for publication as a printed book: spelling corrections, reformatted several examples to fit smaller page width, moved long urls to footnotes to improve line-breaking, added extra index entries. Added this "History" section.

The source code for the original version of this document is available from `ftp.gnu.org/gnu/bash/` in the file 'bash-3.2.tar.gz'.

The source code for this version is available from `http://www.network-theory.co.uk/bash/manual/src/`

A complete set of differences can be obtained from the same location.

Index of Shell Builtin Commands

Index of Shell Reserved Words

Parameter and Variable Index

Function Index

Y

Concept Index

I

J

K

L

M

N

O

P

Q

R

S

Printed in the United Kingdom
by Lightning Source UK Ltd.
134519UK00002B/164/A